From a Pastor's Heart

Kenneth Hagin Jr.

From a Pastor's Heart

Kenneth Hagin Jr.

Unless otherwise indicated, all Scripture quotations are taken from the *King James Version* of the Bible.

Scripture quotations marked AMPLIFIED are taken from *The Amplified Bible*. Copyright © 1987 by The Zondervan Corporation and the Lockman Foundation, Grand Rapids, Michigan. Used by permission.

Scripture quotations marked NEW INTERNATIONAL VERSION are taken from *The Holy Bible, New International Version*. Copyright © 1978 by the Zondervan Bible Publishers, Grand Rapids, Michigan. Used by permission.

First Printing 2000

ISBN 0-89276-740-5

In the U.S. write:
Kenneth Hagin Ministries
P.O. Box 50126
Tulsa, OK 74150-0126
1-888-28-FAITH
www.rhema.org

In Canada write:
Kenneth Hagin Ministries
P.O. Box 355, Station D
Etobicoke (Toronto), Ontario
Canada, M9A 4X3

Contents

III. OBEDIENCE

IV. PEACE

V. REVIVAL

VI. VICTORY

Preface

Dear Friend,

Have you ever encountered a situation and wondered, *What am I going to do?* If you have, you are not alone. We have all felt like that at one time or another. I have faced trying times in my life and wondered if anyone really cared.

There are times in life in which you will encounter trials that seem overwhelming. And the devil will take the opportunity at that low moment in your life to distract you and confuse you and get you looking at the problem instead of the truth that is found in the Word of God.

When you are being attacked by the enemy, you don't need someone to speak harshly to you or give you a list of all the things that you need to do. No, you need someone to minister the love of God's Word to you. And that's what this book intends to do — to give you a needed word of encouragement in due season.

As a pastor, I see the hurts and struggles that people are going through. And I know that the same sincere Word of God that has carried me through every situation in my life will also carry you through as well. It wasn't the Word spoken to me harshly or with condemnation that helped me. No, it was the Word of God spoken to me in love.

My prayer is that as you read this book, your heart will be encouraged and strengthened in the love that comes from God and His Word. No matter what you may be facing in life, God cares about you and desires to minister to you. Allow the Word of God in this book to minister to you, because the Word you receive comes to you in love — straight from a pastor's heart.

Kenneth Hagin Jr

INSPIRED WORDS

CONCERNING

Destiny

FOR THE SEASONS

OF YOUR LIFE

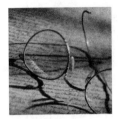

Changing Your Thinking

T"This book of the law shall not depart out of thy mouth; but thou shalt MEDITATE therein day and night, that thou mayest observe to do according to all that is written therein: for then thou shalt make thy way PROSPEROUS, and then thou shalt have GOOD SUCCESS."

— Joshua 1:8

Why does meditating on the Bible bring success? Because the Bible contains God's thoughts, and we need *His* thoughts. Our thoughts are small, weak, and limited to what we've learned and experienced in life. Our thoughts can actually hold us in bondage!

Many times our thoughts can be inaccurate because we don't know the whole matter. They can also be filled with fear

1

and failure. But if we are in Christ, there is no need for us to have any fear!

Study the great men and women of the Bible. Every time these great faith giants of God stayed with God and made His thinking their own, they prospered. But every time they began to think their own thoughts and became fearful, they got into trouble.

You see, our human thoughts are limited. But God is not limited in knowledge, wisdom, foresight, understanding, or experience. He knows everything, so He's not limited in any way!

Therefore, we need to lose our negative thinking, and get the mind of Christ! Philippians 2:5 says, *"Let this mind be in you, which was also in Christ Jesus."* When we have the mind of Christ, we are thinking God's thoughts. And as we think God's way according to His Word, our lives are changed.

We live beneath our privileges in Christ when we continue to think our own thoughts — thoughts of fear and failure! But we stop living beneath our privileges in Christ when we begin to realize what belongs to us in God. That's why we need to let God's thoughts saturate our minds in every area of our lives.

Many Christians are good natural thinkers, but God wants us to be *supernatural* thinkers. Yes, we live in the natural.

But because we are born again, we can also think supernaturally. So lose your carnal, worry-filled natural thinking and become a success in God!

According to Joshua 1:8, it's only as we meditate on God's thoughts that we become successful. Thinking like God does brings us into prosperity in every realm of life! I want you to notice something else about that verse. It says that you are the one who makes your own way prosperous! So if you want to be prosperous, think like God does! When you start thinking God's thoughts, you'll even get rid of attitude problems.

Lose your small thinking and get God's big thinking. Lose your negative thoughts and get God's positive, faith-filled thoughts. The mind of Christ is not something impossible to attain. As you begin to meditate in the Word, your thinking will be transformed. You'll begin to think big just like God does. Change your thinking, and you'll change your life!

When we have the
mind of Christ,
we are thinking
God's thoughts.
And as we think
God's way according
to His Word,
our lives are changed.

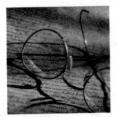

Choosing What To Say

FROM A PASTOR'S HEART

"*A man's belly shall be satisfied with the* FRUIT OF HIS MOUTH; *and with the* INCREASE OF HIS LIPS *shall he be* FILLED.

DEATH *and* LIFE *are in the* POWER OF THE TONGUE: *and they that love it shall eat the fruit thereof* [whether good or evil]."

— Proverbs 18:20-21

There is tremendous power in words — written words, spoken words, and words set to music. Words will lead you along the right path, or they will take you down the wrong path.

One translation of Proverbs 18:21 says, "Death and life are determined by the tongue." Therefore, people who are

5

always speaking negative words will eventually receive the consequences their words produce — failure, defeat, and sorrow.

You see, words are containers. They can be filled with ungodliness — hate, doubt, fear, and unbelief. Or they can be filled with godliness — love, joy, peace, happiness, and faith. Words can curse, or words can bless. Words can discourage, or they can encourage. Words can wound, or they can make whole.

Words filled with the power of God will linger with you and literally change your life. The words you hear will either help you along life's path or hinder you!

Words can build confidence into people, or words can destroy faith and confidence in people. Biting, stinging words spoken in the morning by a husband or a wife can rob them both of efficiency throughout the day. But loving, tender, and beautiful words will fill their day with strength that leads them to victory.

Why is it that some families grow up strong and stable, always winning in life? One reason is that right words were spoken at home. The atmosphere in your home is a product of your words. What are you building into your children? Are you building failure and defeat? Or are you building success and victory?

You cannot afford to talk failure. You cannot afford to talk doubt, unbelief, fear, and dread. Negative words register on your heart, building failure into your life. And these words can take control of your life. Few of us realize the power of our words.

You cannot afford to tell the story you heard the other day about So-and-so and then hope to succeed in God. Don't poison other people's ears as yours have been poisoned. Instead, let your words be used to comfort and bless others by ministering grace, blessing, and encouragement.

It is vitally important what you say about yourself and others! Every day you are faced with this crucial decision: "What do I choose to say today? How can I fashion my words to determine my future today? Will I build up those around me, or will I tear them down with my words?"

Be a wise steward of your words! Base your words on what God's Word says, so that wonderful things can happen in your life. Begin now to determine that your future will be filled with faith, love, and success — because your words contain the power and the grace of God!

Words filled with the
power of God will linger
with you and literally
change your life.
The words you hear will
either help you along life's
path or hinder you!

Developing a Vision for Your Life

F R O M A P A S T O R ' S H E A R T

"Where there is no vision, the people perish . . . ."

— Proverbs 29:18

Vision can be defined as *the sense of sight, the power to see or to perceive by imagination,* or *something seen in a dream.* It can be a supernatural idea from God, or it can be a goal that you set for yourself. But one thing is clear: if you do not have a vision, you're not going to have any success in life.

When I was in high school, I used to run track. Back in those days, I could run the 100-yard dash in 10 seconds flat (the world record was 9.8!). I could cover some ground in a hurry!

But even though I was considered to be a top sprinter, I knew I had to build up more strength in my legs and increase my

9

wind capacity in order to stay on top. So I worked on accomplishing those things.

When practice was over and my teammates were taking their showers, I'd take another thirty minutes and run a series of 220s. When the others had finished for the night, I continued to train and practice. Why? Because I had a goal in mind — to win first place in all of my events!

Now whether you realize it or not, everyone is dominated by vision, both spiritually and naturally. You are either looking toward something — making the proper confessions and doing the things that will get you to your goal — or you're looking back at how good things used to be.

Well, God does not particularly care about using people who are constantly looking back. Remember what happened to Lot's wife when she looked back? She became a chunk of salt standing beside the road (Gen. 19:26)!

No, God is interested in your accomplishing something. He wants you to be successful.

You see, whatever vision you get ahold of — that's what pushes or drives you forward to achieve your goal. That's why you must have a vision for something that is out in the future instead of always looking back. For example, if you're sick, you have to have a vision of yourself being well, not getting sicker. If you're in need, you have to envision yourself with all of your needs met, not with more needs. You have to see yourself as you want to be.

I'm talking about having a vision for your life. Maybe you had a vision for your life once, but it has become dimmed or stifled by adverse situations. Then I encourage you today to begin looking to Christ for all of your answers. It doesn't matter what your circumstances may be. Quit looking at everything around you, and begin to fasten your eyes on Jesus!

Maybe God has spoken to your heart about some things you're to do, or you just have a personal goal you want to accomplish in life. That's good. Stir up that vision, and let it dominate your life so that it invigorates and stimulates you to pursue your goal. Then start making the proper confessions and commitments that will help you attain that vision.

You see, it's not enough to just have a vision; you also have to become committed to it. If there is no commitment to the vision, then there will be no success.

How do you stay committed to the vision? You keep your eyes on your goal, you get the Word of God in your mouth, and then you go for the gold!

Friend, I want you to know that you can be a success according to the Word of God — when you have vision for your life!

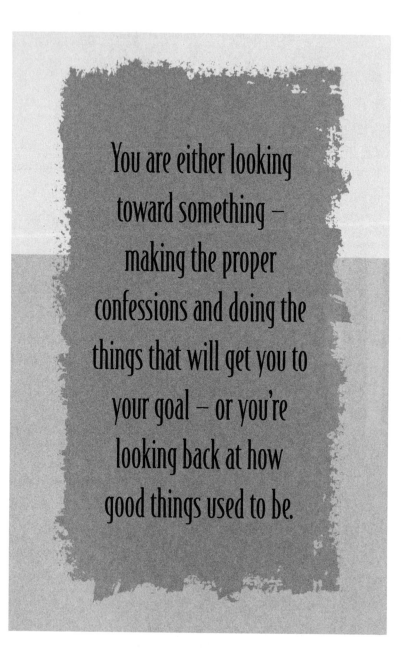

You are either looking
toward something –
making the proper
confessions and doing the
things that will get you to
your goal – or you're
looking back at how
good things used to be.

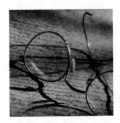

Drawing Near to God

"Draw nigh to God, and he will draw nigh to you . . . ."

— James 4:8

Have you ever arrived early at a meeting or event and observed the different people as they entered the building? It's interesting to watch how some folks choose a seat in the back of the room, while others head straight for the front as soon as they enter the building. Why is that? Because they want to get as close as they can to where the action is going to be.

It seems the farther away you get from whatever is happening, the more distractions there are, and the more you miss. But the *closer* you get to an event or happening, the *less* distractions there are, and the more you get out of it.

The same is true in following God. Some have a hard time living for God, because they stay at the back of the building, just inside the door.

You see, when you're not living close to God, it's easy for the devil to wave flags, tap you on the shoulder, or do whatever else he can to distract you. But the closer you move toward God, the more difficult it is for the enemy to get you tangled up in peripheral things that can cause you to miss out on God's blessings.

So you should desire to live as close to God as you can. Every day you ought to be getting closer to His throne, pressing into the plan He has for your life and delighting yourself in the Lord.

But you can't delight yourself in the Presence of the Lord by hanging way out on the outer fringe.

For example, I play golf, and I can tell you that there's not much to get excited about when you're on the fringe of the green. You may be twenty feet away from the hole, and there isn't any delight in that — that's a tough shot!

But you can sure delight when your ball is just a half-inch away from the hole, because that's a sure shot. You'd almost have to get run over by a golf cart not to make it. I mean, you just barely have to tap the ball, and it will fall in!

You see, a golfer has joy and delight when he gets up close to the hole on the green. And that's the way we should be when it comes to the things of God. We need to be delighting in the fact that we're in the Kingdom by getting close to God — by getting right up front, near His throne.

I don't know about you, but I intend to draw closer to God every day. The Word says, *"Delight thyself also in the Lord; and he shall give thee the desires of thine heart"* (Ps. 37:4). So I'm going to keep building myself up on my most holy faith by praying in the Holy Spirit (Jude 20). And I'm going to keep speaking to myself in psalms, hymns, and spiritual songs, delighting in the Presence of the Lord.

We all have the opportunity of drawing nearer to God. So come on in, and move up to the front row. Draw near unto God, and He will draw near unto you!

The closer you move
toward God, the more
difficult it is for the
enemy to get you tangled
up in peripheral things
that can cause you to miss
out on God's blessings.

Experiencing Feelings of Uncertainty

Any time you step out and obey God's direction for your life, at some point in your journey of faith you will probably experience feelings of uncertainty and mixed emotions about your future. But when you are walking by faith and trusting God to direct you step-by-step, you won't always see the whole picture at once. You will probably only see glimpses of the plan God has for you like pieces to a puzzle.

In the Old Testament, God led His people, but they had to trust Him and obey Him every step of the way in order to fulfill His will and receive His blessing. For example, God instructed the children of Israel to carefully follow the Ark of the Covenant so He could lead them into their Promised Land — a land of prosperity and rich blessings. They were instructed when they saw the Ark of the Covenant to move from the place they had settled and

17

"go after it" (Joshua 3:3). Joshua commanded the people not to follow the Ark too closely, nor to lag behind ". . . *that ye may know the way by which ye must go: FOR YE HAVE NOT PASSED THIS WAY HERETOFORE*" (Joshua 3:4).

The children of Israel traveled paths uncharted as they journeyed by faith toward their destiny. They had to depend solely on the Lord for direction because they had not gone that way before. Similarly, under the New Covenant, God has set a course before each of us. But in order to fulfill our destiny in Christ, we must obey God and trust Him to guide us step-by-step in our walk with Him.

As you follow the Lord's direction for your life, the future won't always seem clear to you, and God's plan for your life will not unfold overnight. Payday in God's Kingdom doesn't always come every Saturday night. But it does come! In the long run, obedience to God and His Word always pays.

In your walk with God, you will travel paths you haven't traveled before — paths that are new and unfamiliar to you. But they are not new or unfamiliar to God. The Bible says God knows the way that we take (Job 23:10) and that darkness is as light to Him (Ps. 139:12). You may not know the future, but God does! He has a plan for your life, and He knows how to successfully lead you in order to accomplish His plan.

As a Christian, you do not face the future alone. Jesus, the Good Shepherd, is with you, and He will not lead you on a path where harm will overtake you. Rather, He promises to gently lead you on *right* paths if you will trust and obey Him. The Lord may lead you on a path where the enemy seems to lurk on every side, trying to steal your joy and get you out of faith. But as you faithfully follow the Good Shepherd, you will receive your promised reward and feast at the table of blessing God has prepared for you (Ps. 23:5).

We must choose whether to follow God's leading and direction for our lives or our own plan. Will we allow Jesus our Shepherd to guide us by His Spirit, or will we follow the path of our own design? We may not know everything the Lord has in store for us, but if we will trust Him and obey His leading every step of the way, He will bring us into our own promised land and fulfill His plan for our lives.

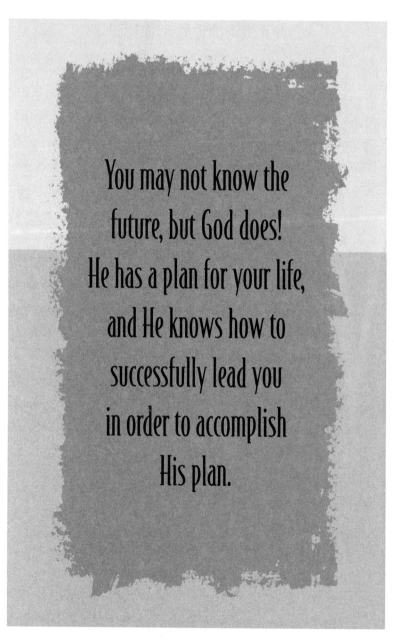

You may not know the
future, but God does!
He has a plan for your life,
and He knows how to
successfully lead you
in order to accomplish
His plan.

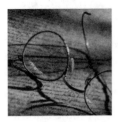

Facing a Crossroad in Life

F R O M   A   P A S T O R ' S   H E A R T

Crossroads. Everyone encounters them in life. A crossroad is a place of decision that will affect the course of one's life. Jacob faced a crossroad when he wrestled with the angel at Peniel (Gen. 32:24). Jesus Christ faced a crossroad when He struggled with His own soul in the Garden of Gethsemane (Matt. 26:36-42).

Crossroads. North or south, east or west, which course will you choose? Which path will you take — God's will or your own ways? The choice is up to you.

In Proverbs 3:5 and 6, King Solomon wrote: *"Trust in the Lord with all thine heart; and lean not unto thine own understanding. In all thy ways acknowledge him, and he shall direct thy paths."*

When you face a crossroad in life, you need to wait on God until you can move forward with confidence that *God* is directing your path. The Bible says, *"There is a way which seemeth right unto a man, but the end thereof are the ways of death"* (Prov. 14:12).

Just because a certain path or course of action *seems* right, that is no guarantee it *is* right. And just because another path may seem unpleasant or contrary to what we would think is best does not mean it is wrong. Therefore, we must trust in the Lord and not lean to our own understanding or insight. We must rest assured that God knows the end from the beginning, and He will lead us in the way that is best for us.

None of us can afford to rely upon our own understanding. Because of our finite nature, we are limited. Even what we see and what we think we know can be very different from what is actually true. Only an all-wise, an all-knowing, and an all-loving God can be trusted to provide the very best for us in every area of our lives.

Each of us must ask ourselves one important question when we face a crossroad in life: Will the path we choose be a path that will fulfill God's plan for our lives? Or will it simply be a path that follows our own reasoning for what we want out of life?

When you choose to obey the will of God for your life, you put yourself in a position to hear and to receive God's guidance for the course and direction of your life. Obedience to God will keep you calm in the midst of chaos and will bring you through to victory in the face of defeat. But true obedience must be more than just a one-time action; obedience must be a lifestyle.

In true obedience, the element of humility is always present. I don't mean the *false* humility people "put on" in order to influence what others might think of them. I mean humility that is from the heart. Genuine humility is the result of true obedience, and humility keeps your heart tender and pliable before God so that you are always willing to say, "Lord, not my will, but Thy will be done."

Crossroads. Places of decision. If you walk in obedience before God day-by-day, moment-by-moment, you will be sensitive to the Holy Spirit's leading and instruction for you. Obedience increases the anointing of the Holy Spirit and expands the measure of God's grace upon your life. Disobedience decreases the anointing and limits the measure of grace you operate in.

If you make the decision to obey God — no matter what you may see, think, or feel — when you stand at a crossroad in your life, you will be able to hear the still, small voice of the Holy Spirit say, "*. . . This is the way, walk ye in it . . .*" (Isa. 30:21).

When you face a
crossroad in life,
you need to wait on
God until you can
move forward with
confidence that
God is directing
your path.

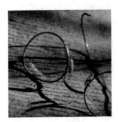

Fulfilling God's Purpose

FROM A PASTOR'S HEART

In Ecclesiastes 3:11, *The Amplified Bible* says that God has set eternity in the heart of every man: ". . . He also has planted eternity in men's hearts and minds [a divinely implanted sense of a purpose working through the ages which nothing under the sun, but God alone, can satisfy]. . . ."

This verse applies to both sinner and saint. For the unsaved person, the "eternity" God has set in man's heart is the longing he has for a Savior and the need he has to know God's love. For the Christian, I believe the divinely implanted purpose of God is for him to demonstrate God's love for the world by sharing the Savior, Jesus Christ, with the lost. No matter what a Christian's station or calling in life, God's ultimate purpose for every believer is to reach lost and dying souls and win them for His Kingdom.

From the moment our redemption was consummated by the Lord Jesus Christ, God's plan for all men was that they come into the knowledge of the truth and be reconciled to Him through His Son, Jesus Christ. And that plan, God's Great Commission, included preaching the good news of man's redemption to every creature — to every man, woman, boy, and girl on the earth.

Through Jesus, God made provision for every person on earth to be reconciled to Himself. Because of the sacrifice of His Son Jesus, the Bible says God is not holding men's trespasses against them (2 Cor. 5:19)! That's the good news of redemption that we are to proclaim to the lost in our own world, in our own sphere of influence in life. As Christ's ambassadors, taking His Place on the earth, we are to urge men everywhere: *Be reconciled to God!*

I believe every Christian has a God-given yearning or desire to reach out to the lost and bring them into fellowship with the Father. But that desire must be cultivated through prayer in order for it to produce fruit — a harvest of souls for God's Kingdom.

Matthew 7:7 says, *"ASK, and it shall be given you; SEEK, and ye shall find; KNOCK, and it shall be opened unto you."* Our desire to fulfill God's purpose prompts us to *ask* Him for souls — for the heathen as our inheritance (Ps. 2:8). As we diligently *seek* the Lord, He clothes us with His glory and molds us into vessels of honor, meet for His use (2 Tim. 2:21). And as we *knock*, those doors of opportunity are opened to us to share the good news of the Gospel in our own world.

The heart of a soulwinner is not the possession of just a few in the Body of Christ. We have a promise from Jesus Himself that as we follow on to know Him, He would make us fishers of men (Matt. 4:19; Mark 1:17). As we follow our Lord and Savior Jesus Christ, walking in the light of His Word, He Himself will teach us to catch men — to win souls — for His Kingdom.

We must earnestly seek God so that He may cultivate within us the heart of a soulwinner. The Bible says, ". . . *they that turn many to righteousness* [shall shine] *as the stars for ever and ever*" (Dan. 12:3), and ". . . *he that winneth souls is wise*" (Prov. 11:30). As we hold forth the Word of Life to those around us, we as Christians can proclaim the truth that there is a Heaven to gain and a hell to shun; we can turn many to righteousness to the glory of God.

No matter what a
Christian's station or
calling in life,
God's ultimate purpose
for every believer is
to reach lost and
dying souls and win
them for His Kingdom.

Making a Decision

"Multitudes, multitudes in the valley of decision . . . ."
— Joel 3:14

Today many people are in the valley of decision. In fact, every day of our lives, we all make decisions that affect our destinies and the course of our lives.

The choices you and I make in life are vitally important because our destinies in life are determined by the choices and decisions we make. We either choose God, or we choose the devil. We either choose life, or we choose death (Deut. 30:19). It's our decision. There is no middle ground.

Friend, each one of us has to willfully make the decision to live for God and to walk with Him. Joshua said, *". . . as for me and my house, we will serve the Lord"* (Joshua 24:15). Each one of us has to make the choice to turn our back on evil and serve the Lord with our whole heart.

Are you at a crossroads in your life? Have you determined in your heart to put God first? Your choice will dictate the rest of your life. If you'll put God and His will first in your life, you can be sure to make the right decisions!

Some people refuse to make any choice because they are afraid of failing. But sometimes when a person doesn't make a choice, he is already choosing failure. Sometimes no choice is a choice!

It is said that entrepreneurs Henry Ford and J. C. Penney failed many times before they finally attained success. You see, it wasn't failure that dictated their future. No, their ultimate success was dictated by their decision: "Nothing can stop me! I will succeed!"

Therefore, do not allow the fear of making a decision paralyze you. You don't have to bounce from one crisis to another and vacillate from one decision to another. You can succeed! But you will have to take a stand for God and stand firm in your decision to serve Him.

Have *you* been caught in indecision because of fear? Remember, you don't have to make your decisions alone. Turn to God, and He will give you the wisdom and strength to make every decision — large or small.

What are you going to do with your life spiritually? Are you going to be afraid to make a decision for God? Are you going to make decisions based on what people think? Or are you going to make your decisions based on what God's Word says?

If you are already saved but seem to be hindered in making spiritual progress, don't just sit there! Get up and begin doing something for God. God promised in His Word, "Whatever you put your hand to I'll prosper" (Deut. 28:8; Ps. 1:1-3). Put your hand to something! Reach out to help others. Serve God's people. Be a blessing to someone else!

Some of you are facing decisions in the natural. You'll have to allow God to lead and guide you to the right decision. It's going to take some extra time spent in prayer with God so He can speak to your heart. Stay open to God and let Him lead and guide you in His Word. Some people already have their minds made up, so they couldn't hear from God if He shouted!

Multitudes are in the valley of decision. Don't halt between two opinions! Choose God. Choose the will of God. Choose the things of God. Go with God. Do what God is telling you to do. The decision is yours.

The choices you and I
make in life are vitally
important because our
destinies in life are
determined by the choices
and decisions we make.

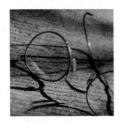

Preparing for Tomorrow

"Joshua told the people, 'Consecrate yourselves, for *tomorrow* the Lord will do amazing things among you.'"

— Joshua 3:5 (*NIV*)

Many times people say, "I'm not thinking about tomorrow; I'm just living day by day." But do you realize that what happens to you tomorrow depends on what you do today?

For example, say you're planning to go on a church trip, and the bus is scheduled to leave promptly at five o'clock on Saturday morning. However, instead of getting everything ready for the trip on Friday, you decide to do it the morning of the trip. Then on Saturday morning, you accidentally wake up late! So you scramble around to get ready, but by the time you get to the church, the bus has already left. Well, guess what? If you'd taken care of things on Friday when it was "today," you would have been ready for "tomorrow"!

That's one reason so many people end up in trouble spiritually — they never prepare for tomorrow with their faith. They don't continue to study the Word. They don't continue to maintain fellowship with God in prayer.

No, we need to get ready spiritually today for what the Lord wants to do tomorrow!

Notice that Joshua said to the people, "Consecrate yourselves." That's the first step towards a successful tomorrow — consecration. What does that mean? It means to set yourself apart, to be submitted to God "lock, stock, and barrel," as we'd say in Texas. In other words, it means to be fully devoted to God in everything.

In order to consecrate yourself, you have to get rid of "excess baggage" in your life.

When I was in the Army, all the recruits were issued military packs that we had to carry around on our backs during field drills. Those packs were filled with all sorts of gear — C rations, a canteen, a change of clothes, a first-aid kit, half of a shelter tent — just about anything we would need out in the field. But when it came time to conduct certain training exercises, we got rid of those backpacks in a hurry. Why? Because we didn't want anything slowing us down. We had to outrun bullets, and we needed to move as fast as possible!

You see, when a soldier is out on the battlefield in the heat of battle, he gets rid of everything he can that will hinder him. Yet some folks are engaged in spiritual battles, trying to fight the good fight of faith, but they have all kinds of excess baggage weighing them down!

No, get rid of anything that will hold you back spiritually. Get rid of fear, anger, ill will, unforgiveness, hatred, and so forth. Those things are "excess baggage," and they will hinder you in running your Christian race. If you don't get rid of them today, they will affect you spiritually tomorrow.

For instance, how many times have you heard someone say, "I'm going to start my diet tomorrow"? But then that "tomorrow" never comes, and the person never loses the weight that he said he would. I remember that I had been saying for years that I was going to lose some weight and start an exercise program. Then one day I stopped and said, "No, I'm not *going* to start; I *am* starting! My tomorrow begins today!"

Friend, what you do today will affect where you are tomorrow. Your tomorrow has to begin today in your personal life. You can't live a worldly lifestyle and tell off-colored jokes today and expect to be spiritually strong tomorrow. You can't forsake assembling together with other believers today and expect to be spiritually strong tomorrow. You can't run with the wrong crowd today, befriending those who serve the world, without it affecting your spiritual life tomorrow.

Your tomorrow also has to begin today in your home. If you want to establish true, godly relationships with your husband, wife, or children, you have to begin today — not tomorrow.

And your tomorrow has to begin today in the church, because the success of your local church depends upon the success of your own personal life. A chain is only as physically strong as its weakest link, and a church is only as spiritually strong as its weakest member!

Friend, you are not here just to exist. You are building a life. If you build your life upon the wrong ideals and the wrong principles, you won't stand the test of time. But if you build it upon the principles and values of the Word of God today, then you're preparing for a successful life tomorrow.

The decision is yours. The Lord will do amazing things in *your* life if you will consecrate yourself and get yourself ready for success — because your tomorrow begins today!

Friend, what you do
today will affect where
you are tomorrow.
Your tomorrow has
to begin today in
your personal life.

Preparing for Your Vision

F R O M   A   P A S T O R ' S   H E A R T

"Where there is no vision, the people perish . . . ."

— Proverbs 29:18

Vision is the sense of sight, but it is also the power to perceive in your heart what is not yet manifested in the natural realm. Vision can be a goal in your heart — something you want to accomplish in the future — or it can be a supernatural vision or dream God put in your heart.

Some people call "vision" goal-setting. When you have a vision for something you want to achieve, you set goals to attain it. Having a vision will help you succeed in life!

Use God's Word to *see* yourself as a success in life, and as a result, receive whatever you need from God. Once you find scriptures in the Word that promise you what you desire, meditate

39

on those scriptures until they become real in your heart and mind. And then act in faith to bring those goals and dreams to pass.

You can talk about your vision and your plan of action to bring your vision to pass, but the time will come when you must step out in faith. Until you commit to bring your dreams to pass, your goals will probably remain just that — dreams.

Some people have no plans, no goals, and no dreams. They get up in the morning, go to work, come home — and that's the extent of their lives. They just do the same thing over and over again without any thought for the future, without even planning for the future. Really, they aren't *living*; they are just *existing*. They may have dreams in their hearts, but they haven't done anything to bring those dreams to pass.

You see, you've got to be committed to do your part to bring the dream God gave you to pass. And God will do *His* part. It will take your commitment not only in the spiritual realm, but also in the natural realm. Determination, discipline, and perseverance are all needed to accomplish your dream.

The Bible mentions the person who just talks but doesn't put any action to his faith. Faith without works is dead (James 2:20,26). And then the person who starts to take action but wavers is called *double-minded.* Because he wavers back and forth, he doesn't accomplish anything.

You'll have to put some action to the dream God gave you! Your vision must dominate your life. You won't be able to accomplish your dreams if you just float through life with no plan or purpose for the things you do. If you haven't set any goals to succeed, you probably won't succeed. Take time to analyze your goals. Then determine a plan — the best way to bring those goals to pass.

People are dominated by some kind of vision, whether they realize it or not. Some people allow negative things to dominate them. Others allow their God-given dreams to motivate them, and they work with God to bring that vision to pass.

You can have the most wonderful dream from God burning in your heart, but if you don't do anything in the natural to prepare for that dream, nothing will happen. God is always faithful to do His part! So what are *you* going to do with the dream God gave you?

You can talk
about your vision and
your plan of action
to bring your
vision to pass,
but the time will come
when you must
step out in faith.

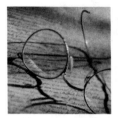

Tempted To Look Back

F R O M   A   P A S T O R ' S   H E A R T

"With the coming of the dawn, the angels urged Lot, saying, 'Hurry! Take your wife and your two daughters who are here, or you will be swept away when the city is punished. . . .'

As soon as they [the angels of the Lord] had brought them out, one of them said, 'Flee for your lives! Don't look back, and don't stop . . . .'"

— Genesis 19:15,17 (NIV)

These scriptures refer to the deliverance of Lot and his family just before God destroyed the wicked cities of Sodom and Gomorrah. The angel told Lot's family, ". . . Don't look back, and don't stop . . ." (v. 17).

There's a spiritual principle in these scriptures we can each learn from. It's the principle of not looking back to the failures of the past, but looking ahead to the brightness of the future, as we pursue our God-given dreams.

As I read these scriptures, I am reminded of Moses and the children of Israel at the Red Sea. God had just delivered them from the bondage of Egypt. But when the Israelites got as far as the Red Sea, they realized Pharaoh and his army were in swift pursuit, trying to take them captive again (Exod. 13:18-22; 14:1-9).

The Israelites found themselves at a crossroad! They could obey God and continue journeying to their promised land. Or they could disobey God, be recaptured by Pharaoh's Egyptian army, and be subjected once again to the bondage of the past.

The children of Israel couldn't afford to look back — or even to linger — or they would forfeit the promised blessing. If the Israelites were to obtain victory, they couldn't afford to look in *any* direction but straight ahead to what God had promised them!

When the circumstances of life encompass you, set your face like flint on Jesus, the Author and Finisher of your faith (Heb. 12:2). He will guide you safely to victory! If failure and defeat try to dog your tracks, and if bondages of the past try to haunt you, just keep looking to Jesus and to the joy God has set before you in His Word. With God, the future can be bright with promise and hope!

The Bible says, ". . . *lift up the hands which hang down, and the feeble knees; And make straight paths for your feet* . . ." (Heb. 12:12,13). In other words, keep marching straight ahead to victory! Keep your feet firmly planted on the pathway to victory and your eyes riveted on the promised blessing. You can obtain your dreams in God if you won't look back and you won't quit!

When the circumstances
of life encompass you,
set your face like flint
on Jesus, the Author and
Finisher of your faith.
He will guide you
safely to victory!

INSPIRED WORDS

CONCERNING

Faith

FOR THE SEASONS

OF YOUR LIFE

Believing God

FROM A PASTOR'S HEART

All of the promises God ever made from the time of Creation until now are for us today! God's character absolutely guarantees that what He promised shall be done. On the other hand, a dishonest man may make a promise that he doesn't intend to keep. Or, an honest man may make a promise that he cannot keep. A man may even make a promise but die before he has a chance to fulfill it.

Well, God not only has the ability and the disposition to keep every promise He's ever made, but He also *cannot* and *will not* lie (Heb. 6:18)! Therefore, there is no possibility that the promises He has made to you will not come to pass in your life.

The Word of God says in Matthew 24:35, *"Heaven and earth shall pass away, but my [Jesus'] words shall not pass away."*

That means that whatever God said in His Word is still true today. If in the Old Testament God sent His Word and healed His children's diseases, then the Word of God will still heal His children today!

Do you believe that God parted the Red Sea, that He sent fire from Heaven to guide the children of Israel, and that He gave them manna, quail, and water when they didn't have anything to eat or drink? Well, just believing all the things that God did in the Old Testament, or even the things that Jesus did in the New Testament, is not enough. You must believe that God can do them *today*! You must believe that He is the same right now as He has always been.

The Lord does not change (Mal. 3:6); He is the same yesterday, today, and forever (Heb. 13:8). Many people are looking for a new revelation. But the only revelation that you need is that Jesus is the same today as He has always been. When you understand that, then you believe that He can and will do today what He did in the past! And what He will do today, He will do tomorrow.

There is a promise in the Word of God for your every need. Whatever your need may be, God's Word has the answer. God promises comfort, healing, deliverance, peace, forgiveness, safety, strength, wisdom — you name it, He has it! And if God has it, *you* can have it!

God said, "I am the Lord that healeth thee" (Exod. 15:26). God's Word says that by Jesus' stripes you were healed (1 Peter 2:24). So it doesn't matter how rich or poor you are, you must simply say in your heart and with your mouth, "I believe God!" And God's promise of healing will work for you.

Healing is just *one* of the 30,000 promises listed in the Bible. The Word of God also says that God will supply all your needs (Phil. 4:19). Do you think God really meant what He said in His Word? Well, if God means what He says, then why are Christians going around sick? Why are they going around poor or powerless?

Notice, I'm putting the responsibility back on *us*. You see, as long as we can jump and shout and get all "hyped" up, everyone thinks it's great. But when the responsibility is on us and when it's up to us to do something about the situation, sometimes we tend to pull back and say, "Well, now I thought we're supposed to pray the *prayer of faith*."

You can pray the prayer of faith, but it won't do you any good unless your faith "reaches out" and "grabs hold" of God's promise. You can have whatever you need from God — regardless of what it is — but *you* have the responsibility of possessing His promise.

Today you may be in a situation like blind Bartimaeus (Mark 10:46-52) — needing a touch from God. You can sit by the road, listen to the crowd, and continue to say, "Lord, please come by here. Lord, help me, please. Oh, Lord, please. You know how I need to be healed." Or you can do what blind Bartimaeus did. You can come to Jesus and receive by faith whatever it is you need.

Whose report will you believe? Will you believe the report of people, doctors, the world, or the devil? Or will you believe God? In His Word, He has already promised to meet your every need. So whatever your need may be today, God has promised the answer. If you want to see His promises fulfilled in your life, start by saying, "I believe God!"

Just believing all the
things that God did
in the Old Testament,
or even the things
that Jesus did in
the New Testament,
is not enough.
You must believe that
God can do them *today*!

Developing Your Faith

". . . *God hath dealt to every man the* MEASURE OF FAITH."

— Romans 12:3

Some Christians want to pray for faith. They don't seem to realize that if they are born again, they are already *believers,* and they already have faith; they just haven't developed it.

Actually, the Bible says that every person is given a measure of faith. It also says that faith comes by hearing the Word of God (Rom. 10:17). So as a believer, you do have faith, but faith has to be exercised so that it can grow and develop.

The same principle is true in the natural realm. For example, if you want to develop your body, you have to exercise and lift weights. There is no use trying to lift 500 pounds if you

55

can't even lift 100 pounds! It could even be dangerous because you might tear a muscle that may take months to heal.

Things work much the same way in the spiritual realm. You are not going to get your faith to work if you don't exercise it. People who haven't taken time to develop their faith have weak faith. So if they try to believe God for something beyond their level of faith, their faith fails them, and they are hindered for months. Then they think they don't have faith when really they have just never *developed* their faith!

If you are a believer, you do have faith. So start where you are in faith. Start believing God where your faith is developed right now.

For example, if you were trying to climb a ladder, would you start at the top rung? No, you'd have to climb the ladder one step at a time, beginning at the bottom rung. No one can take one step and climb to the top rung of a six-foot ladder. But it is very easy to climb a ladder when you take just one step at a time.

It's the same way with faith. Start developing your faith now for the things you need from God. But first you're going to have to know what God has said in His Word. If God hasn't said it, then you can't believe for it. But if He promised you something in His Word, then you can believe Him to bring it to pass in your life. The Bible says, *"God is not a man, that he should lie;*

neither the son of man, that he should repent: HATH HE SAID, and shall he not do it? or hath he spoken, and shall he not make it good?" (Num. 23:19). Whatever God says that you can have, *you can have!*

Faith is not sight. Faith is not feeling. Faith is based on the fact of what "God hath said" in His Word.

Some people confuse faith with feelings. They are always waiting for a feeling before they will believe God. In essence, that is telling God that His Word is a lie. But that's not how faith works. First, you have faith, and then the feelings come.

God promised that if we believe His Word, we can receive from Him (Mark 11:24). So our assurance must be in God's Word. We don't need feelings when we have the facts — the facts of God's Word. If God said it, shall He not do it? He watches over His Word to perform it (Jer. 1:12). He will certainly make His Word good in our lives if we will just believe Him!

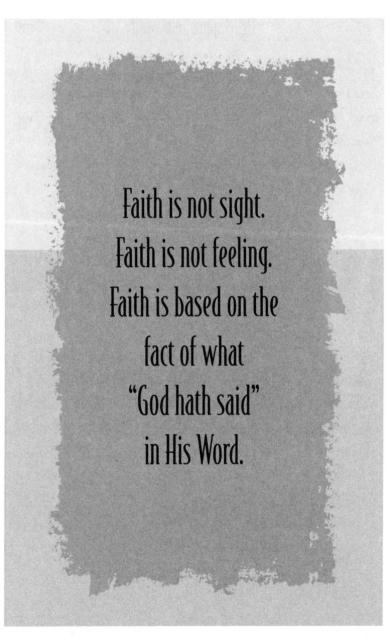

Faith is not sight.
Faith is not feeling.
Faith is based on the
fact of what
"God hath said"
in His Word.

Facing an Impossible Situation

FROM A PASTOR'S HEART

"*. . . The things which are impossible with men are possible with God.*"

— Luke 18:27

Jesus Christ, the Son of God, spoke these words to His disciples. But did you know that He is still speaking these words to *you* today?

I'm sure that many times you've been confronted with situations and circumstances that have seemed impossible and insurmountable to you. Many times you may have felt that God spoke to you about something He wanted you to do, but the natural circumstances seemed to scream at you, "It's impossible! You can't do it!" Maybe even well-meaning people told you, "You can't do that! It's impossible!"

But I read in my Bible that the God of the impossible says, "I can do *all* things. Whatever you need, I can do it! Nothing is impossible with Me!" In Jeremiah 32:27, God said, *"Behold, I am the Lord, the God of all flesh: is there any thing too hard for me?"*

So before you consider the natural circumstances, consider the God of the impossible whom you serve. God can't fail you. No circumstance is too hard for Him. The God of the impossible laughs at difficulties.

So when you're overwhelmed with thoughts of failure and the words of people telling you that you can't succeed, look to God! Don't be hindered by thoughts of doubt or people's words. I don't know about you, but I choose to believe God rather than doubt and unbelief. Some of you just need to believe God rather than the circumstances!

Sometimes people ask, "What's going to happen to us believers in a world of instability?"

When people ask me questions like that, I am reminded of several million people in the Old Testament whom God called *His* people. He fed, clothed, and took care of them in the middle of the wilderness for forty years!

If God can take care of them, He can take care of us. God hasn't changed! His wonder-working power is still available to those who trust Him.

People may call us simple-minded if we dare to believe God and take Him at His Word. But I believe that nothing is impossible to the God of the impossible!

Every day as you walk upon this earth, you will be faced with the decision to believe either God or the adverse circumstances. You will have to make the decision to believe that the God of the impossible can cause you to succeed in life. You'll have to believe God rather than the doubt and unbelief you hear in the world.

If you are being driven and buffeted by the trials of life, I challenge you to believe God in the face of every opposing obstacle. Dare to declare with the Apostle Paul, "I believe God that it shall be even as it was told me" (Acts 27:25).

Proclaim to the world that what the God of the impossible has said in His Word, He is able to perform! Stand on the promise of God: *"For with God nothing shall be impossible"* (Luke 1:37).

When you're overwhelmed with thoughts of failure and the words of people telling you that you can't succeed, look to God!

Faith Seems Weak

"Acquaint now yourself with Him [agree with God and show yourself to be conformed to His will] and be at peace; by that [you shall prosper and great] good shall come to you."

— Job 22:21 (*Amplified*)

There is a vast difference between merely knowing *about* God and actually *knowing* Him. Theologians may quote many profound doctrinal truths about God and His mighty acts. They may even spend numerous hours of diligent study to acquire information about Him. However, knowledge of God and His ways is not gained through intense study *about* Him. Rather, knowledge of God is gained by intimate fellowship *with* Him.

Strong fellowship with God is the very foundation of strong faith in God. You become personally acquainted with God through His Word, through His Spirit, and through time spent with Him in prayer and worship. When you come to know God in a personal, intimate way, you become confident in His goodness and mercy, and you become confident in His ability and His willingness to meet your needs. And that confidence is faith.

Through the years, having ministered both as an evangelist and also as a pastor, I have listened to people make what they thought were confessions of faith. They would quote a long list of scriptures, and then recite what they were believing for.

But sometimes there was a certain shallowness in their statements and in the way they made them. Their words revealed more emphasis upon *what* they were believing for, instead of reliance upon the One *in whom* they were believing. It seemed these people were actually trying to convince themselves of the truth, instead of sharing true heart-felt convictions. It was no surprise to me when they eventually wrote me or called to say, "I believed God for such-and-such to happen, but it didn't."

That kind of "believing" is not faith. At best it's hope; at worst it's presumption. Faith comes by hearing the Word of God (Rom. 10:17). But faith must also be acted upon and developed.

And strong faith is developed through an active, personal acquaintance with a personal God — not through impersonal, methodical manipulation of principles.

You need to know the principles of God's Word, and it is important to memorize scriptures. However, it doesn't matter how many scriptures you can quote; if you don't know the God of the Scriptures, you're missing it! Don't stop short by acquiring only a knowledge about God and His Word. Move on to *know* God.

When you accept Jesus Christ as your Savior, you are born again into a relationship with the living God. You become a child of God the Father. But after you become a child of God, it's up to you to cultivate fellowship with God. It's up to you to become acquainted with your Heavenly Father.

When you draw near to God, His Word assures you that He will draw near to you (James 4:8). Decide now that you will draw near to God by esteeming and obeying His Word and by entering into His Presence through prayer, praise, and worship. I encourage you to make a decision in your own heart right now that you will become better acquainted with God. When you do, your life will be enriched beyond measure.

Knowledge of God
and His ways is not
gained through intense
study *about* Him.
Rather, knowledge of
God is gained by
intimate fellowship
with Him.

Focusing on the 'Ifs' in Your Life

"Then said Martha to Jesus, Lord, IF thou hadst been here, my brother had not died. . . .

Jesus saith unto her, Said I not unto thee, that, IF thou wouldest believe, thou shouldest see the glory of God?"

— John 11:21,40

"If" is a small word that some people say we shouldn't use. But I want to look at a different side of the word "if." Did you know that the "ifs" in your life can become your triumphs — *if* you will only believe God?

That's what Jesus told Martha. He said, "If you would only believe, you would see the glory of God." God can take any situation in your life and turn it around to your good — *if* you'll only trust Him and believe that He is able to do it.

No matter what circumstance you face in life, God can turn it around! You hear people say all the time, "If only I'd done this or that," "If only my folks had treated me differently," or "If only I hadn't been born on the wrong side of the tracks." Probably every person on earth has some "What ifs" and "If onlys" in his or her life.

But when you focus on the "ifs" in your life, you are hindering your own success. Instead of looking at the negative circumstances in your life all the time, why not focus on the positive circumstances? Focus on what you *do* have — not on what you don't have. What are your assets? What are your talents? Make use of what you have, and commit to God what you don't have.

Learn to change your "ifs" to possibilities rather than to impossibilities. Learn to change the negatives to positives. Then instead of being hindered in life by the "What ifs" and eventually failing, you will find yourself succeeding.

Actually, the "ifs" in your life give you a great opportunity to prove that the Word of God works. You can organize your defeat into victory. It's your responsibility to take the Word of God and stand on the promises of God so He can turn every "If only" and "What if" into a victory!

A woman once said to a minister, "If only my family weren't like they are. They mock me for trying to live for God. If only you understood my circumstances."

This preacher looked at her and said, "Never mind about your circumstances. Put *God* between you and your circumstances!"

The woman returned a few days later and said to the minister, "You know, I found out that if I would change the 'If only' in my life to 'If only I would believe,' everything would change."

God can change those defeats in your life and turn them into victories! God can take any situation and turn it around. Instead of dwelling on the negative side of "if," get on the positive side of "if" — *if* you will believe, you will see the glory of God!

When you focus on
the "ifs" in your life,
you are hindering your
own success. Instead of
looking at the negative
circumstances in your life
all the time, why not
focus on the positive
circumstances?

Implementing the Law of Faith

F R O M   A   P A S T O R ' S   H E A R T

"For verily I say unto you, That whosoever shall say unto this mountain, Be thou removed, and be thou cast into the sea; and shall not doubt in his heart, but shall believe that those things which he saith shall come to pass; he shall have whatsoever he saith."

— Mark 11:23

I want you to notice three important truths in this verse of Scripture: If you don't doubt in your heart, but believe that the things you say are going to come to pass, you can have what you say.

In other words, if what you say with your mouth is a result of what you believe in your heart, then your faith will work for you. That is God's inevitable law of faith.

71

This truth is woven throughout the New Testament in all of the apostles' writings. In fact, a person can't even receive salvation without this faith. Romans 10:9 and 10 is the basic scriptural principle to receiving salvation — believe in your heart that Jesus Christ is Lord and say it with your mouth. That's God's inevitable law of faith!

However, what you are believing God for is not going to fall on you like ripe cherries falling off a tree. It doesn't work that way. *You* have to do something. You have to declare what you want based on God's Word and not look at anything else. Then watch it happen! That's how you put God's inevitable law of faith to work in your life.

You can choose to speak the Word over your situation — that's called a *good* confession. Or you can speak the negative things about your situation. The Bible calls that an evil report. Anytime you speak negative words about your circumstances, it's an evil report.

Notice I didn't say, "Don't *state* facts." Or "Don't *face* facts." You can state the facts and you can face the facts. You can say, "Yes, this is the way it is." But then you have to move on from there because when you're in faith, the situation doesn't have to dictate your present or future circumstances.

You don't have to be moved by what you see. You don't have to be moved by the circumstances. You may come up against negative circumstances and negative facts, but with the eye of faith, you can look through the circumstances and through the facts to the victory on the other side. To do that, your faith and your confession must be in line with God's Word, not in line with the circumstances.

You see, the eye of faith always sees the victory. The eye of faith always presses through negative reports, negative facts, and negative circumstances to the victory on the other side. Circumstances have nothing to do with the eye of faith. Why? Because faith is not so concerned with what *is* as it is with what *can be.*

Faith sees the situation, all right. It notices it and says, "Yes, it's there." But then true faith goes on to state what the Word of God says about the situation.

When you're in faith, you will notice the circumstances, but then you'll declare: "The *Word of God* says I am more than a conqueror. The *Word* says nothing is impossible with God. The *Word* says I am more than a victor through Christ Jesus who loves me."

Faith in the Word of God takes contrary circumstances and negative facts and turns them around so you come out the victor — every single time. That's God's inevitable law of faith.

If what you say
with your mouth is
a result of what you
believe in your heart,
then your faith
will work for you.
That is God's inevitable
law of faith.

Increasing Your Faith

"And the apostles said unto the Lord, INCREASE OUR FAITH.

And the Lord said, If ye had faith AS A GRAIN OF MUS-TARD SEED, ye might say unto this sycamine tree, Be thou plucked up by the root, and be thou planted in the sea; and it should obey you."

— Luke 17:5,6

Do you know that with God, just a little faith will get you much? How do I know that? Because in Luke 17:6, Jesus didn't say that you had to have faith as a mustard *tree*. He said all you needed was faith as a mustard *seed*! A mustard seed is very small.

In fact, seeds are always smaller than the product they produce. Jesus was telling the disciples that the faith they had was sufficient. That's why when the disciples asked Jesus to increase their faith, He told them that their faith was a seed *that just needed to be planted.*

When you pray, maybe you've thought to yourself, *I just don't have enough faith to believe God!* According to this passage, I think Jesus would probably tell you, "You've got all the faith you need. Just use what you've got! Plant the faith you have, and that's how it will be increased."

You know, many believers are convinced they can't do certain things, so they never try. They're always looking at their own limitations — even their own faith limitations. But God has no limitations. He said, *"Behold, I am the Lord, the God of all flesh: is there any thing too hard for me?"* (Jer. 32:27).

Do you know what that scripture tells me? It says that there's nothing that you and God can't do together. If you'll team up with God and use the faith you have, you and God can move mountains!

Some Christians say, "Oh, I can believe God for the little things in life. But when it comes to believing God for something *big*, I don't have enough faith for that."

But Jesus said, ". . . *If thou canst believe, ALL THINGS are possible to him that believeth*" (Mark 9:23). He didn't say there was a difference between faith for little things and faith for big things.

Maybe you think it takes a lot of faith to believe God. But that's not what *Jesus* said. All you need is faith as a grain of mustard seed.

Therefore, if you have any faith at all, you have enough to receive whatever you need from God. Now all you've got to do is plant the faith you have! How do you plant it? By saying what God's Word says — *that's* standing on the promises of God. Say what God says belongs to you, and keep on saying it!

You don't need lots of faith for bigger faith projects. You simply need to use the faith you have by taking God at His Word and *acting* on it! All it takes to receive from God is a little bit of faith in a great big God!

Maybe you think it
takes a lot of faith
to believe God.
But that's not what
Jesus said.
All you need is faith
as a grain of
mustard seed.

Ministering Salvation To the Elderly

F R O M   A   P A S T O R ' S   H E A R T

A letter came across my desk once from a concerned gentleman who had tried unsuccessfully to lead an elderly woman to Christ. The elderly woman objected to the salvation message on the basis that it is more difficult for an older person to be saved than it is for a younger person.

But the Bible says the Gospel ". . . *is the power of God unto salvation to EVERY ONE that believeth . . .*" (Rom. 1:16). The Gospel of salvation that lives and abides forever can effectually transform *any* person, whether he is young or old.

As I read this gentleman's letter, I was reminded of scriptures about God's love and faithfulness to the elderly. For example, Joshua told his people in his last hours on the earth, ". . . *behold, this day I am going the way of all the earth: and ye know in all your hearts and in all your souls, that not one thing hath*

79

failed of all the good things which the Lord your God spake concerning you; ALL ARE COME TO PASS . . . and not one thing hath failed thereof" (Joshua 23:14).

God had given Joshua many victories in his lifetime, both as Moses' servant and later as the leader of God's people. God had always kept His Word to Joshua, and even in Joshua's old age, God didn't forsake him.

While it's true that a person who doesn't know the Lord can become more hardened to the Gospel as he gets older, God's Word is powerful enough to save *anyone* who will believe and act on it. God told the prophet Jeremiah, *"Is not my word like as a fire? . . . and like a hammer that breaketh the rock in pieces?"* (Jer. 23:29). The Word of God can melt even the hardest heart and the most stubborn rock of resistance!

The precious blood of Jesus is not limited by any boundaries of age. No matter how many mistakes you've made or how you've disobeyed God in the past, God is good and rich in mercy to *all* who call upon Him in sincerity. The Bible says God's tender mercies are new every morning, and that His mercy endures forever to anyone who will believe Him (Lam. 3:22-23; Ps. 136:1). That is true for anyone regardless of his age!

Do you believe the good news of the Gospel — that the Savior, Jesus Christ, was crucified and raised from the dead so *you* could be saved? The Bible says, *". . . there is joy in the presence of the angels of God over one sinner that repenteth"* (Luke 15:10). It would do no injustice to the Scriptures to add to that verse: *no matter what his age!*

The eyes of God are on man for good and not for evil from the inception of life until he "goes the way of all the earth" in death. You're never too old to receive eternal life and experience the riches of God's salvation!

No matter how many
mistakes you've made
or how you've disobeyed
God in the past,
God is good and rich in
mercy to *all* who call
upon Him in sincerity.

Mountains Are in Your Way

FROM A PASTOR'S HEART

"*. . . If ye have faith, and doubt not . . . ye shall say unto this mountain, Be thou removed, and be thou cast into the sea; it shall be done.*

And all things, whatsoever ye shall ask in prayer, believing, ye shall receive."

— Matthew 21:21,22

This Scripture passage is talking about moving mountains in prayer. Jesus said that if you pray to God in faith, you can move those mountains or obstacles that try to hinder you from receiving the promises of God in your life.

You may be in the biggest financial mess you've ever been in. You may be sick and afflicted in your body. You may have problems you think are impossible to solve. But you possess

83

within yourself the ability to talk to your loving Heavenly Father who can solve every one of your problems. That ability is called *prayer*.

Prayer is the power that moves mountains! Just wishing and hoping won't get the job done. God is a faithful God who hears and answers prayer. That's why we need to learn the secret of dwelling so closely with God in prayer that He can move those mountains in our lives out of the way.

If you want God to move mountains out of your life — the problems you can't overcome — then you must learn how to pray scripturally and *expect* an answer. The Bible says if you ask, you *shall* receive.

One way people weaken their prayer life is that when they pray to God and don't see an immediate answer, they begin to waver and assume it's not God's will to answer that particular prayer.

But the rules concerning mountain-moving prayer are always the same. If you ask according to God's Word, then you know you've prayed according to God's will (1 John 5:14,15). When your petitions line up with God's will, then you can expect an answer.

Don't waver in your faith just because you don't see the situation change immediately. As soon as you ask in faith, God begins to work behind the scenes on your behalf.

God doesn't want us to be resigned to defeat or failure in any area. He wants us to overcome the difficulties and obstacles in life through prayer that is rooted and grounded solidly on God's Word.

You hold the key to success in your life, because prayer is a *choice*. Are you going to pray to God who holds infinite power in His hands? Or are you going to remain prayerless?

You have the power to move the mountains out of your life by praying to a faithful God who hears and answers prayer! Just pray according to God's Word in faith, expect your answer, and remember — nothing is too hard for your Heavenly Father!

Don't waver in your
faith just because you
don't see the situation
change immediately.
As soon as you
ask in faith,
God begins to work
behind the scenes
on your behalf.

Needing a Miracle

Do you need a miracle? Success comes by *standing* firmly on the promises of God and not wavering. The Bible says that when you've done all to stand — keep on *standing* (Eph. 6:13,14)!

What do I mean by *standing* on God's Word? I mean that in the face of every situation that opposes you, you refuse to quit. Instead, you think on God's Word and believe God's promises to you. You hide the Word in your heart concerning your situation and speak God's Word over your situation until there's a change!

If you quit, you won't gain anything! But if you keep on putting your trust in God, you have everything to gain because the promises in His Word are yours to claim.

Yes, sometimes circumstances come against you, and you have to stand on the Word in the face of some overwhelming obstacles. But what have you got to lose by standing on God's promises? Take God at His Word because He's faithful and His Word never fails (Isa. 55:11; Matt. 24:35).

Many of you have been standing and standing for something, and you think it's never going to come to pass. But that's just the devil's lie. Maybe you've hindered your answer from coming to pass by wavering concerning God's promise to you.

Faith is believing what *God said*. It's that simple. Did God promise you something in His Word? Are you going to believe what God told you and stand your ground against the devil and adverse circumstances? Or are you just going to give up and let the devil steal what God promised you?

God has already given you your answer in His Word. Now it's up to you to appropriate what you need by faith in His Word. You do that by standing your ground on the Word even when it seems like every circumstance is against you.

Circumstances are nothing to God! According to God's Word, every knee must bow to Him, and that includes every contrary circumstance too. But you must cooperate with God by developing faith in your heart and speaking faith with your mouth.

Don't think or speak contrary to what God has promised you. Feed your mind on the promises in God's Word so you can stand strong in the midst of any storm or circumstance that might try to assail you.

God has not forsaken you. He's waiting for you to take Him at His Word and hold fast to your confession of faith by standing strong on His Word. His Word will prosper in any situation. When you stand your ground on His promises, you won't have to give up in despair and quit because His Word will prosper, and you'll see your answer!

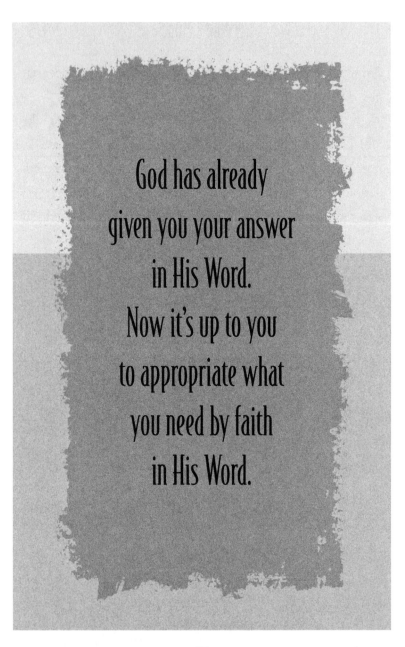

God has already
given you your answer
in His Word.
Now it's up to you
to appropriate what
you need by faith
in His Word.

Receiving What Belongs to You

"According as his divine power hath given unto us all things that pertain unto life and godliness, through the knowledge of him that hath called us to glory and virtue."

— 2 Peter 1:3

If a person helping you with a project hands you a tool that you need to work with, what would be your natural response? Most likely, you'd say "Thank you" and take it.

Well, when the Word of God tells you that God has given you everything you need for life and godliness, how should you respond? Just thank Him for it, and take it!

Aren't you glad God didn't say He was *going to* give you the tools that you'll need or He *might* give them to you if you pray hard enough? No, He said He *has* given you all things that pertain unto life and godliness — that means whatever you need to succeed in life, both *naturally* and *spiritually*!

I think too many people try to divorce their natural life from their spiritual life. They put natural things in one category and spiritual things in another. But if you stop to think about it, you are a natural person and a spirit being at the same time, living in a physical body. So it's possible for the natural and the spiritual to work together.

That's why you'll find many of the same principles that make you a success in the natural realm can also work for you in the spiritual realm.

For example, how many successful businessmen do you know who just sit in their office with their feet propped on their desk and have had big business deals automatically fall in their lap? You probably don't know any — because a successful businessman doesn't sit down and wait for business to come to him. He goes out and gets it!

Well, in the same way, the blessings that belong to you in the spiritual realm won't just fall on you like ripe cherries off a tree, as my father would say. You have to *take* them!

You see, even though Jesus Christ has already won the victory, that doesn't necessarily mean you are reaping the benefits of it. And even though Jesus has given the Church — the called-out ones who have been born again by His precious blood —

authority over sickness, poverty and lack, and everything that's contrary to the Word of God, that doesn't mean that you're living in total health and prosperity and enjoying your full redemptive rights!

You have an adversary that wants to steal every promise of God away from you that he can. He'll try to trick you into sitting around on the pew or in your home, never doing anything because you're "waiting on the Lord."

The devil will try to deceive you into believing that love, joy, peace, and happiness will be yours in the "Sweet By-and-by." But what good is it to look toward Heaven to enjoy the blessings of God when you're alive down here now? No, you need a little bit of Heaven *now* to go to Heaven with!

Don't misunderstand me. I thank God for the future and the glorious hope that we have in Christ. But *now* is when we need food on our tables and clothes on our bodies, not when we get to Heaven.

We need to be able to give people God's Word of hope and encouragement *right now* — when the world is going through an energy crisis, an economic crisis, an ecological crisis, and every other kind of crisis you can think of!

So I want to encourage you. Don't just sit idly by and allow the enemy to steal what rightfully belongs to you. Raise the bloodstained banner of the Lord Jesus Christ in your life!

Wave it in front of the enemy, and let him know that *you* know Jesus Christ has already defeated him.

Friend, God has already given you everything you need to make it in this life. So get up, reach out with your faith, and take what God says is yours now!

The blessings that
belong to you
in the spiritual realm
won't just fall
on you like ripe
cherries off a tree,
as my father would say.
You have to *take* them!

Things Go Wrong

How do you cope with life when things go wrong? For instance, what should you do when someone you know dies and goes home to be with the Lord even though you prayed and believed for his healing? What do you do when you pray and the answer doesn't seem to come?

These are questions we all have to deal with in life. How we respond to adversity determines the quality of our spiritual life. We have a decision to make when situations occur in life that we don't understand. We can choose to become stronger in God by believing that Heaven and earth will pass away, but God's Word will never fail (Matt. 24:35). Or we can lose our faith in God and just go through the motions of Christianity.

Sometimes when people don't understand things that happen in life, they try to figure it out in their own human reasoning. For instance, when someone fails to receive healing, some people come to the conclusion, "Well, it must not be God's will to heal everyone." But conclusions that cause you to take sides against the Word of God are dangerous!

We can't afford to let conclusions like that get into our mind and determine our thinking. Are we going to get our eyes on the *situation* or on God's Word? According to the Word of God, Jesus Christ bore our sicknesses in His own body, and by His stripes we are healed!

Sometimes when loved ones don't get healed, people even blame themselves by saying, "If only I'd prayed and fasted more, maybe he wouldn't have died." But you can "maybe" yourself into a state of confusion that can cost you your own walk with God!

The Bible says that in this life we see through a glass darkly (1 Cor. 13:12). Some translations say we see dimly as through a mirror. We don't always see everything distinctly or understand fully everything that happens in life, but God does.

So, friends, one thing we need to settle in our hearts is that there is never a problem with the Power Source! God's Word is true, and the power in His Word doesn't change because God doesn't change.

Make the decision you're going to meditate on the Word and believe what the Word says, not what circumstances look like. Otherwise, the enemy will bring up every possible idea and notion to get you to discount and doubt God's Word. If he can confuse your mind, he can steal your joy. If he can steal your joy, he can steal your peace. Lack of joy and peace produce weak faith. Then you've really got a problem because it takes faith to please God!

We can't alter biblical doctrine to fit circumstances and experiences! We don't form doctrine on circumstances; we form our doctrine on what the Word says. And the Bible says Jesus Christ doesn't change (Heb. 13:8), and neither does His Word!

Really, in every perplexing situation, your answer is God Himself. He knows and understands all things, so just commit those situations to Him. Make the decision to believe God's Word, regardless of circumstances.

Talk to your Heavenly Father. Tell Him, "Lord, I don't understand this situation, but You do. So I'm turning this over to You, and I won't even touch it again in my thought life. I make the decision to walk with You and to walk by Your Word. Come what may, Your Word is true!"

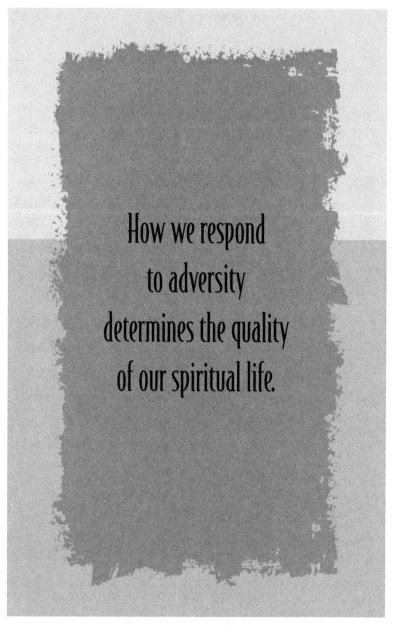

How we respond
to adversity
determines the quality
of our spiritual life.

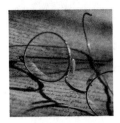

Waiting on God

God never said that we wouldn't have tests and trials. But He did promise us in Isaiah 40:31 that He would renew our strength if we wait upon Him — if we stay consistently before Him in prayer and in the study of His Word.

"To renew" means to remodel or restore something until it's just like new. If you've ever remodeled an old car, then you know what I'm talking about. You have to pull that old car apart down to its frame and then put it all back together with new parts. You put in a new motor, new brake lines, new electrical wires, new shocks — new everything! Then you redo the whole interior and give the body a fresh paint job. After the car is finished, it looks as if it just came off the assembly line, because it's been completely renewed!

Well, in the same way, we can begin to show a little bit of wear and tear from the everyday stress and strain of living in this world. But we can get into the Word and learn how to get our strength renewed by the power of God.

Isaiah 40:31 says, "... *they that wait upon the Lord shall renew their strength; they shall MOUNT UP with wings as eagles* ...."

Mount up. Those are two good words. Being from Texas, I've ridden plenty of horses. If I rounded up a horse and told you, "Mount up," I'd really be telling you to *get on the horse.* You could stand around all day holding on to the horn of the saddle, but you'd never go anywhere until you actually got on the horse. However, once you *mount up* and get in the saddle, that horse will carry you where you want to go!

There's been many a cowboy who couldn't swim across a wide river, but his horse could carry him to the other side. The same thing is true concerning your walk with God. There are many places you can't go and many things you can't overcome alone. But if you wait upon the Lord and mount up on the wings of the Holy Spirit, so to speak, the Lord will carry you through every test, trial, and temptation until you come out victoriously on the other side!

Waiting upon the Lord doesn't mean you just sit back and do nothing. That's why the Bible says, "they that wait upon the Lord shall *mount up*"!

You see, many times in the midst of a trial or tribulation, people sit back, fold their hands, and do nothing. They say they're waiting on the Lord, yet they're really just trying to justify why they're not taking their responsibility as they should. But God said that He would bless whatever they set their hands to (Deut. 23:20)!

The Lord once said to me, "Many people say they're in faith and they're waiting upon Me when they really aren't at all. Those who are waiting upon Me, those who truly know what faith is and what it means to believe Me, are moving *up* and *out* of their situations."

Friend, have you been waiting upon the Lord concerning a particular need in your life, but it seems as if nothing is happening? You may need to check and see whether or not you've really been waiting upon Him in faith.

Those who truly wait upon God according to the Word won't always remain in the same desperate condition. They may start out in a position of crisis, overwhelmed by problems or circumstances. But as they wait upon God, following His Word and doing what He says, they move out of that position.

So I ask you this question: "What are *you* waiting on?"

Learn to wait upon the Lord. And you'll find that instead of floundering around in a state of weakness, your strength will be renewed, and you'll "mount up on wings as eagles"!

The Lord once
said to me,
"Those who are
waiting upon Me,
those who truly know
what faith is and what
it means to believe Me,
are moving *up* and *out*
of their situations."

You Experience Failure in Life

F R O M   A   P A S T O R ' S   H E A R T

"For ye shall GO OUT with joy, and be LED FORTH with peace. . . . Instead of the thorn shall come up the fir tree, and instead of the brier shall come up the myrtle tree . . . ."

— Isaiah 55:12-13

Are there areas of your life that have been barren and unfruitful, yielding only thorns and briers? Instead of focusing on the failures of your past, picture yourself happily strolling through a vast meadow filled with daffodils and daisies, lush green grass, and fruit-bearing trees of every kind. Then picture the Lord handing you the title deed to the land, saying, "I want you to have this; it's yours."

"It's too good to be true," you might say. But it *is* true! God has called you to enjoy victory in every area of your life in

Christ and to be fruitful in His Kingdom. Jesus said, *"Herein is my Father glorified, that ye bear much fruit . . ."* (John 15:8).

We bear much fruit and bring glory to God when we obtain His promises through faith — by believing and acting upon God's Word. The faith of Abraham, the patriarch of faith, brought glory to God because he refused to waver concerning God's promises. And although once barren and unfruitful, through his faith Abraham obtained his promised blessing (Gen. 12:2; Heb. 6:12,15).

You may be experiencing failure and defeat in some area of your life today, but God wants to turn the barren waste-lands of your life into fruitful meadows! You hold the title deed to a beautiful land — your inheritance in Christ. So turn your back on the failures of your past and turn your praise upward to God. Stir yourself up to believe and act upon God's Word and continually praise and give Him glory.

God is no respecter of persons. What He has done for anyone else, He will also do for you. As you are faithful to believe and act upon God's promises, you will *go out* of your barren land with joy and be *led forth* with peace into a fruitful land of plenty. Instead of the thorn and the brier, the fir and the myrtle trees will spring up in your life, and you will reap a rich harvest of God's blessings.

You may be experiencing failure and defeat in some area of your life today, but God wants to turn the barren wastelands of your life into fruitful meadows!

INSPIRED WORDS

CONCERNING

Obedience

FOR THE SEASONS

OF YOUR LIFE

Choosing To Obey God

H

" . . . Hath the Lord as great delight in burnt offerings and sacrifices, as in obeying the voice of the Lord? Behold, to obey is better than sacrifice, and to hearken than the fat of rams."

— 1 Samuel 15:22

Tremendous blessings come as a result of obeying God. Think about what the world would be like if everyone obeyed everything God said in His Word. If we were all fully obeying God all the time, this world would be Heaven on earth! Our obedience would bring love among mankind and justice to everyone.

However, the reality in today's world is that many believers put their own wills first, not God's will. When we put our own human wills first, we experience envy, malice, war, strife, injustice — and a whole lot of turmoil.

Also, some believers only obey God because they have to — not because they want to. But it's obedience to God from a willing heart that brings the blessings of God into our lives. Those who willingly choose to follow God and obey Him are the ones God rewards.

Once we obey God's will and follow after Him, we find peace instead of turmoil. We find God's justice instead of injustice. We find love and joy instead of malice and strife. And it's in the quiet resting place of obedience to God that we discover God's love.

It's in those times of trusting God obediently from the heart that our faith can flourish and grow. But when we do not obey God, we take ourselves out from underneath the protective hand of God, and we put ourselves in a position where Satan, the god of this world, can operate against us.

Of course, God never walks away from us. We walk away from God when we choose to disobey Him and fail to do what He's told us to do. But obedience to God and His Word brings a rest and a confident trust in Him.

And remember this: God has a greater claim on you than you do! If you've been redeemed by the blood of the Lord Jesus Christ, then you belong to God, and you are no longer lord of your own life — *He* is. You *owe* God your obedience. And it is easier to obey God when you understand the justice and the *rightness* of everything God says and does.

Also remember, we obey God by *faith*. In other words, it isn't always easy. However, it's easier to trust Him when we remember that the God of the impossible is taking care of every situation we face.

It's our choice whether we choose by faith to obey God or to resist Him. The rewards we will receive depend on our decision.

Therefore, you can choose to obey God fully in everything He's told you to do. The rich blessings of God are just waiting on your willing obedience. The Bible says God is not slack concerning His promises. Could it be that God is just waiting for your heartfelt obedience so He can pour out His blessings upon you?

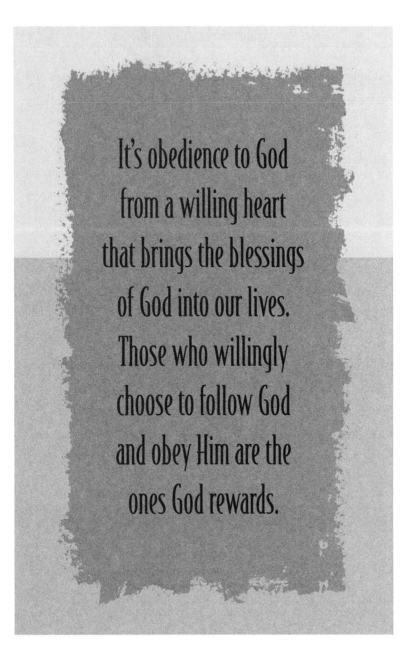

It's obedience to God
from a willing heart
that brings the blessings
of God into our lives.
Those who willingly
choose to follow God
and obey Him are the
ones God rewards.

Experiencing Tests and Trials

". . . I will give her [Israel] back her vineyards, and will make the VALLEY OF ACHOR [trouble] A DOOR OF HOPE. There she will sing as in the days of her youth, as in the day she came up out of Egypt."

— Hosea 2:15 (*NIV*)

The land of Egypt from which the Israelites were delivered is a type of sin to us living under the New Covenant. When you accepted Jesus Christ as your Savior, you too, "came up out of the land of Egypt" — out of the bondage of sin. But since then, perhaps you have found yourself wandering in the wilderness, so to speak, troubled by the tests and trials of life with no hope of a better tomorrow.

We know that God doesn't lead us into tests and trials. But tests and trials come to all of us at one time or another in life. Jesus said, ". . . *In the world ye shall have tribulation . . .*" (John 16:33). But in the same verse, He also said, ". . . *but be of good cheer; I have overcome the world.*"

God wants to bring you out of the wilderness and make your valley of trouble a door of hope! The Bible says that under the Old Covenant, God led the Israelites out of Egypt like sheep and guided them in the wilderness like a flock (Ps. 78:52). The Shepherd who safely led the Israelites out of Egypt and ultimately into their Promised Land is the same Shepherd and eternal Hope who gently guides His flock today.

God said in Hosea 2:14 that He would speak comfortably or tenderly to His people in the wilderness. Through His Word, God is still speaking tenderly to His people today. You may feel like you're going through a dark tunnel because of a test or trial that has beset you. But there is an end in sight! God is saying to you, "Do not fear. Just follow Me and trust Me. It may seem dark, but I know the way, and I will guide you and lead you out."

As you walk obediently with the Lord step-by-step, His Word will be a lamp unto your feet and a light unto your path (Ps. 119:105). And if you will trust in God's unfailing Word, then even in the midst of tests and trials, He will keep you safe on paths of pleasantness and peace that lead onward to victory (Prov. 3:17).

Will you take hold of the hope set before you in God's Word? The Bible says, ". . . *thanks be unto God, which ALWAYS causeth us to triumph in Christ* . . ." (2 Cor. 2:14). Through your faith and obedience to His Word, God can make your valley of trouble a door of hope and expectation. He can bring you out of your dark tunnel of difficulty into a spacious place where rich blessings await you. He can bring you from trouble to triumph!

If you will trust
in God's unfailing Word,
then even in the midst
of tests and trials,
He will keep you safe
on paths of pleasantness
and peace that lead
onward to victory.

Getting Along With Others

Most of the success in our Christian life depends on how well we get along with other people. The Pauline Epistles are filled with scriptures about unity, harmony, and getting along with one another. Several times in the Book of Acts you'll find the statement, "They were all with one accord." When they were in unity and harmony, that was usually when something happened.

Psalm 133:1 says, "How good and pleasant it is when brothers live together in unity!" (*NIV*). But the ability to get along with people usually requires a great deal of effort. It just doesn't happen because you talk about it. Even when everything is going great, you may still have some problems getting along with people.

For example, several years ago a professional football team had been up and down, winning and losing. While they were in a slump one season, a new owner and a new coach were brought in, and the team won the Super Bowl. Then the team won a second Super Bowl. But after winning the second Super Bowl, the coach didn't get a raise from the owner — he got fired!

You see, even though the coach had helped the team win two Super Bowl trophies, he was fired because he rubbed the owner the wrong way! Everything was going great — the team had risen to the top of their game. And yet because of a personal conflict, someone got fired.

When conflicts arise, you can either take the low road or the high road. You can take the low road and wallow in the mire, allowing bad feelings or offenses to pull you down. Or you can take the high road and rise up, living above the situation. By taking the high road, you choose to walk according to what the Word of God says.

God gives us a recipe for getting along with others when we become born again. First Peter 5:5 talks about being clothed with humility. Some of us need to take off the garments we have on and begin to clothe ourselves with compassion, kindness, humility, gentleness, and patience. Then we need to make sure to put on the belt of love, which holds it all together.

If the Lord tarries His coming, we're going to need these garments as we go through life, because the enemy is going to put on the pressure more and more. So we must learn how to live and act like Christians.

There is a slogan that many youth are using: "WWJD" — What Would Jesus Do? It is supposed to remind them to think about what Jesus would do in a situation so that they'll make the right decisions when they receive peer pressure in certain areas. But sometimes I think adults need to pay attention to "WWJD" as well!

Maybe we need to think "WWJS" — What Would Jesus Say? Then rather than saying what *we'd* like to say in certain situations, we'd "let the *Word of Christ* dwell in us richly" and help keep peace in the situation rather than making it worse.

The way we respond to certain circumstances can keep a volatile situation from happening. It depends on our attitude. So we have a choice. We can either do what God says, or we can follow our feelings or what others say.

By taking the high road and choosing to live in unity and harmony, I firmly believe we can make a difference and begin to see more happen in our churches, on our jobs, and in our families. It's when we get out of unity and harmony that the Spirit of God can't flow.

So always let the peace of God rule in your heart. Clothe yourself in humility, compassion, forgiveness, patience, gentleness, and love. And remember "WWJD" and "WWJS" so that when you're in one of life's hard places, you can take the high road!

By taking the high road
and choosing to live in
unity and harmony,
I firmly believe we can
make a difference and
begin to see more happen
in our churches,
on our jobs, and
in our families.

Helping Your Pastor

God placed pastors in the Church *"For the perfecting of the saints, for the work of the ministry, for the edifying of the body of Christ"* (Eph. 4:12). But part of the pastor's mission as head of the *local* church is to fulfill the vision God gives him for his particular locality.

No pastor can carry out God's plan alone. He needs the help of loyal people who are supportive of his vision, willing to work in unity and harmony with him, and committed to the local church — because it takes everyone working together to get the job done!

Speaking as a pastor, my staff and I could not accomplish God's purpose for RHEMA Bible Church without the help of all the members who volunteer and get involved.

Sometimes I like to think of God's plan for the functioning of the local church as a jigsaw puzzle. A jigsaw puzzle has many pieces of different shapes and colors. Some pieces make up the border — the structure or the frame — and the other pieces are designed to fit inside that frame. But all the pieces are made to fit together in a particular way to create a picture that can't be seen in each individual piece alone.

I once worked on a 3,000-piece jigsaw puzzle, and the first thing I did was find all the border pieces. Then I started putting together the frame, fitting as many pieces as I could into their proper places.

I eventually filled in enough of the puzzle to be able to recognize what the picture was supposed to be. But there were still several gaps from the pieces I hadn't hooked up yet. (Those missing pieces were lying off to the side, not doing me any good!) I even had whole segments of puzzle pieces joined together, ready to fill an empty space. But I couldn't fit *them* in until the *other* pieces were in place!

Now that's a good illustration of how some believers are in relation to a local church: they're like the missing pieces of a puzzle. They're off by themselves, not in fellowship with any local assembly and not committed to any particular work.

Perhaps they decided they didn't need to attend a church — that they could just get by listening to a radio or television preacher. Well, those believers are outside the framework that God intended. They aren't "hooked up," taking their place in the structure of an established work and contributing to the plan of God for that church. In fact, their absence could even indirectly be hindering *others* from finding their proper place in a local body!

You see, every piece of a puzzle is important; if even one piece is missing, the picture won't be complete! And in much the same way, *your* presence, talents, and service are needed to complete the overall picture or vision of a local church.

Friend, I want you to realize that you are important to God's plan for the local church and that there is a place no one else but you can fill. I don't know what your place is; that's between you and God. But the important thing is that you find your place, get in it, and serve God faithfully in that capacity.

I believe that as we all find our proper position in the "puzzle," getting in the place where God wants us to be in the local church, we will present a beautiful picture of Jesus Christ to the world.

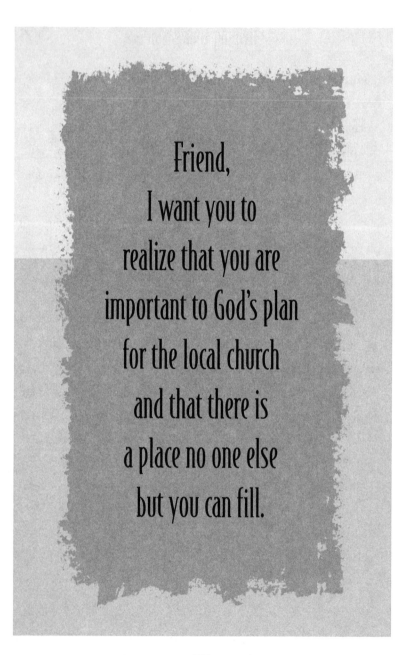

Friend,
I want you to
realize that you are
important to God's plan
for the local church
and that there is
a place no one else
but you can fill.

Hiding God's Word in Your Heart

"This is the covenant I will make with them after that time, says the Lord. I will put my laws in their hearts, and I will write them on their minds."

— Hebrews 10:16 (*NIV*)

What sort of influence is guiding our lives? What makes us tick? We all have maxims that we base our lives upon or words that we live by. Throughout the years, many different things have been said to all of us. They may be sayings or phrases that we learned while growing up or while going to school. But we should also have Scripture that guides us and directs our lives.

Why is it that some people grow up to become strong individuals who conquer life? It might be due to what was instilled in them by their parents. Maybe as children they were always told that they can and will succeed in life.

Well, once a person starts to believe he can be someone and do something in life, then he really can! The problem is that many people have been told the wrong thing — and they began to believe it! So their lives reflect their wrong thinking.

Maybe they were told that they were nothing, that they weren't worth anything, or that they'd never be a success in life. So what did they do? They went and acted out those expectations because that's what was in them.

As the saying goes, *What goes IN is what comes OUT!* Take a look at a sponge. If you put a sponge in clear water and then squeeze it, clear water comes out. But if you take that same sponge and wipe up a bunch of oil and grease and then squeeze it, dirty-looking junk will come out. Why? Because that's what went into it!

Whatever goes into you is what will come out of you when you're under pressure. If your life is filled with gossip, pornography, drunkenness, drug abuse, anger, pettiness, and negative things that tear down rather than build up, when you start getting "squeezed" by the pressures of life — all that garbage will come out.

But if your life is filled with love, mercy, forgiveness, the Word of God, prayer, songs of praise and worship, and the grace

of God, when the pressures of life come and you're squeezed —
out will come the love, mercy, grace, and so forth.

So it's important that you build your life upon what the
Word of God says. You need to understand that it's the things
that are "written" in your mind and heart that control your life.

God has made a covenant with you. If you will study
His Word, He will put His laws into your heart (Heb. 10:16).
And Jesus said, "If you remain in me and my words remain in
you, ask whatever you wish, and it will be given you" (John 15:7
NIV). Well, how are His words going to remain in you unless
you put them there in the first place!

It's the Word of God in your heart and on your mind
that will carry you through when the pressure inevitably comes.
So pay attention to what you're putting on the inside of you
spiritually.

You need to understand that what you take in is what
you're going to put out! You're either going to put out God's Word:
"Thank God, all my needs are met according to His riches in
glory," "By His stripes I'm healed," and so on. Or else you're going
to say, "Oh, my Lord, why did You let this happen to me?" It just
depends on what you've been looking at and who you've been listening to.

It's your choice. You can choose to dwell on the hurtful
things that others have done or said until you become a sponge

that's "full of nothing." But when the pressures of life come, you'll only hinder yourself and others. Or you can hide God's words inside your heart until they become a part of your mind as well. And when somebody does you wrong, love and forgiveness comes out of you. When someone has made a mistake, grace and mercy comes out of you!

So make a decision today to hide God's Word in your heart and become a sponge that is full of His Word and His power. Then when the pressures of life begin to squeeze you, no matter what anybody else says or does, nothing's going to come out of you except courage, love, faith, and power!

It's important that
you build your life
upon what the
Word of God says.
You need to understand
that it's the things
that are "written" in
your mind and heart
that control your life.

Keeping Your Priorities In Order

Family issues have always drawn national attention as people have realized the importance of the family. But in spite of all the dialogue and social programs that have been developed, many families are still dysfunctional.

If you take a look at the busy schedules of some families today, you'll notice how much things have changed over the years. Mom, Dad, and the kids are all running in separate directions, and the home is just a sleeping place where everyone says "hi" while passing one another like ships in the night.

Even in more so-called conservative families, it seems that money, cars, and houses have taken a more important role in people's lives than their children. But those materialistic possessions aren't worth much compared to the reward parents could enjoy through investing in their own children.

Thank God for material blessings and the opportunity to increase in goods and wealth. I am a parent and a grandparent, and I understand the desire of wanting to provide the best for your children. But you could give your children all the luxuries this world has to offer, and it still wouldn't be enough — because your kids would rather have *you*.

If you asked your children what they would desire most if they could have anything they wanted, their answer might surprise you. I've found that most kids would rather have your time and support instead of the latest toys and games. They would rather have your presence at one of their school functions or extra-curricular activities than all the gifts money could buy.

I will never forget one Tuesday afternoon years ago when doctors called me to a conference table and said, "Your son has a brain tumor almost the size of your fist." Stunned, I pushed back from the table and walked over to a corner of the room, where I stood for a moment in complete silence.

To be truthful, at the time of this crisis, I had almost gotten caught up into believing God for this thing and that thing. And thank God, we *can* believe God to have nice, material possessions according to the Word. I'm not against that, but I want you to understand — at that particular moment — those things meant *nothing* to me!

I remember I just put my head in the crevice of those two walls and began to pray. Of course, you know the end of the story: Today my son Craig has two sons of his own, and he is in the ministry, preaching the Gospel. But I began to see something very important that day. I realized that I could take every car I had purchased, every suit I had owned, every dollar bill I had saved — every material thing I ever possessed in life — and they still could never replace my son! Yet, sometimes as parents, we take these things for granted and put our focus on the wrong things.

Aside from God, nothing is more important than our families. I really believe that. The media can talk about restoring family values all they want, but it's not going to come through legislation or government programs. It will only come about as people make the decision to get back to doing what God said concerning their homes.

God didn't create dysfunctional families — people did. And if our home lives are out of order, we as parents have to point the finger right back at ourselves. It's *our* responsibility to make sure our homes are functioning the way that God intended. So let's stop, take a good look at our priorities, and start putting our focus back where it belongs — on the family!

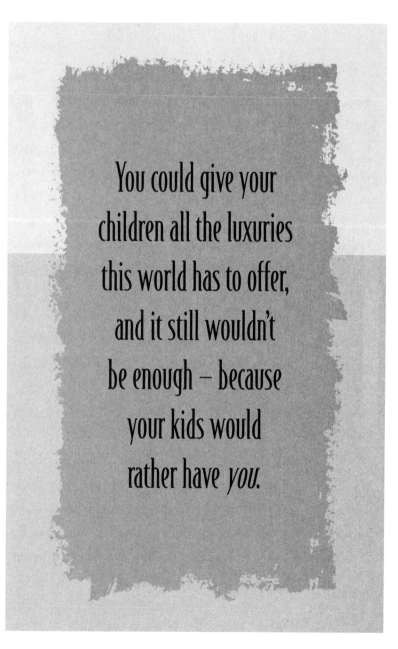

You could give your
children all the luxuries
this world has to offer,
and it still wouldn't
be enough – because
your kids would
rather have *you*.

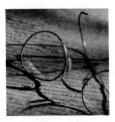

Loving Jesus More Than Anything Else

FROM A PASTOR'S HEART

"So when they had dined, Jesus saith to Simon Peter, Simon, son of Jonas, LOVEST THOU ME MORE THAN THESE? He saith unto him, Yea, Lord; thou knowest that I love thee. . . ."

— John 21:15

This incident between Jesus and Peter occurred right before Jesus ascended to Heaven to sit down at the right hand of God the Father. This was Jesus' last recorded dialogue with Peter who would later become one of the leaders of the Early Church.

There is a strong message contained in Jesus' dialogue with Peter. And each one of us can benefit from asking ourselves the same question that Jesus asked Peter: ". . . *lovest thou me more than these? . . .*"

What did Jesus mean when He said "more than these"? He could have meant, "Peter, do you love Me more than you love your friends, your family, or the other disciples?" Or Jesus could have meant, "Do you love Me more than you love these boats, these fishing nets, and this profession and lifestyle?"

You see, Peter had gone back to fishing for *fish* rather than for *men*. He and the other disciples had been out all night fishing, and they hadn't caught anything. So Jesus could have meant, "Do you love Me enough to give up all this so you can follow Me and preach the gospel?"

"Lovest thou Me?" That's a very searching question, friend. I want to ask you the same question. Do you love Jesus? I'm sure you would immediately answer, "Oh, yes, of course I love Jesus!"

But when you ask yourself that question, then ask yourself, "What are the 'more than these' in my life?" The secret of service to the Lord Jesus Christ lies in the answer to the question, "Do you love Jesus more than anything else in the world?"

No matter how much you know, how much you do, how much you talk, or how much you work to show that you have a great belief in God — if you don't love Jesus with all your heart, all your works don't count for a thing.

I believe if we really love Jesus, we will follow Him with all of our heart. If we really love Jesus, we will want to be like Him. And if we want to be like Him, that will change the way we think, speak, and act. It will change what we do and where we go.

If we love Jesus, then we must remember that Jesus is the One who told us, "Follow *Me*." We can't follow our own opinions, plans, and desires and still faithfully follow Jesus.

It's our responsibility as believers to follow Jesus wherever He may lead us. If we love Jesus, we will say to Him, "Jesus, I'll go wherever *You* want me to go. I'll say whatever *You* want me to say. And I'll do whatever *You* want me to do."

If Jesus Christ Himself looked you in the eyes and asked you, "Lovest thou Me more than these?" what would be *your* answer? Do you love Jesus more than anything else in the world? Jesus gave His life because of His great love for you. Can you do any less than love Him "more than these"?

No matter how much you know, how much you do, how much you talk, or how much you work to show that you have a great belief in God – if you don't love Jesus with all your heart, all your works don't count for a thing.

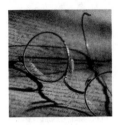

Marching to the Heartbeat of God

F R O M   A   P A S T O R ' S   H E A R T

If you've ever watched a military squadron during a marching exercise, you know that sometimes the soldiers march in rhythm to the beating of a drum. By listening to the beat of a drum, the soldiers are able to march together in perfect unison.

In much the same way, the Body of Christ should strive to march in perfect harmony with the will and purpose of God for the Church. God's ultimate purpose is to reap an abundant harvest of men's souls before Jesus returns.

To accomplish this goal takes *vision, commitment, obedience,* and *unity.* We must live constantly aware of our commission to share Jesus Christ with the world, and we must be committed to that vision both in our personal lives and collectively as the Body of Christ.

We must find out what God wants us to do and obey that. We must hasten to the harvest confident that we are taking our place in this great work and doing our part to fulfill God's plans and purposes in the earth.

God's plan is a victory plan! We as the Church have only to obey God's Voice wholeheartedly and join together to carry out the Master's work. Disputing about doctrinal issues and deviating from the call of God because of spiritual tangents and fad teachings can have no place in the Church if we are to succeed.

Outreach is the heartbeat of the Church because it's the heartbeat of God. Just as the Apostle Paul answered the cry of a Macedonian man to come and help his people (Acts 16:9), let us each be eager to reach out to those yet in darkness with the good news of Jesus Christ. The task before us demands the total efforts of each one of us. So let us march in unison to the heartbeat of God and fulfill God's Great Commission to our generation.

We must live constantly aware of our commission to share Jesus Christ with the world, and we must be committed to that vision both in our personal lives and collectively as the Body of Christ.

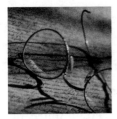

Nurturing the Love of God

"And the Lord make you to INCREASE and ABOUND in LOVE one toward another, and toward all men, even as we do toward you."

— 1 Thessalonians 3:12

Have you discovered that God's love grows in your heart when you nurture and cultivate it in your life? But it doesn't just happen; it takes some effort on your part. Developing the love of God in your heart is just like nurturing and growing a garden. When you have a garden, you have to take care of the tender little plants that are just starting to grow and sprout.

For example, did you ever just plant a tomato seedling in the ground and then go off and leave it? No, if you did, it would wilt and die. If tender little plants are going to grow properly

147

so they can produce a harvest, they must be cared for and cultivated.

The fruit of God's love in us works the same way. The
love of God has been shed abroad in our hearts, but it has to be
cared for, cultivated, and nurtured. There are certain things we
can do to help our love grow.

For example, we've got to water the love in our hearts
by spending time in God's Word and in prayer. Then we've got
to pull out the weeds of selfishness and self-centeredness so our
love can be free to develop. And we've got to nurture and take
care of that love by putting others before ourselves.

You and I have a responsibility if we are going to grow
and increase in God's love! For example, when I was a child, my
grandpa had a garden in his yard. When it rained, the sun would
bake that north central Texas blackland soil until it had a hard
crust on it. My grandpa would go up and down those rows of
plants with his hoe loosening the soil around the plants so the
hardened clay wouldn't choke the life out of the plants.

If the surface of the soil was hard, then when it rained,
the moisture would just run off that hard surface. But if the soil
was broken up so it wasn't hard, the rain would soak into the
ground so the plants could grow.

Many of us are like that hardened soil. Our hearts have
gotten hard! But if we want the love of God in us to produce a

harvest, then we must make sure the ground of our heart is continually soft, not hard, so the love of God can grow unhindered. We must also make sure that there are no weeds that will sap the life from God's love in our hearts.

To grow in the love of God in our lives, we need to continually cultivate the ground of our hearts to make sure our hearts don't get hard. It is so easy to get hard-hearted in life and allow our love to dry up and be choked out by the cares of this life. It's so easy to just go around trying to walk in faith and quoting faith scriptures, but without any love accompanying our faith because our hearts have gotten hard.

So cultivate the love of God in your life! Soften the ground of your heart by saturating your thinking with God's love. Every time someone wrongs you, instead of thinking on that person's bad qualities, choose to think on the good. Replace negative thoughts by quoting the Word. And as you diligently weed negative thoughts and attitudes out of your heart, you'll create a garden in your heart that only produces a harvest of God's blessing!

If we want the
love of God in us
to produce a harvest,
then we must make sure
the ground of our heart
is continually soft,
not hard,
so the love of God
can grow unhindered.

Prospering in Life

F R O M   A   P A S T O R ' S   H E A R T

"This book of the law shall not depart out of thy mouth; but thou shalt meditate therein day and night, that thou mayest observe to do according to all that is written therein: for THEN THOU SHALT MAKE THY WAY PROSPEROUS, and THEN THOU SHALT HAVE GOOD SUCCESS."

— Joshua 1:8

The word "meditate" in this verse means to think about the Word and practice it so that it becomes part of you. You fill your heart and mind with the Word by meditating on the Word, by giving attention to the Word. And to give attention to the Word of God means to think about it continually, mulling it over in your mind!

151

But I want you to notice that after you meditate on the Word, you still aren't guaranteed success. Then you must "... DO *according to all that is written therein!* ..."

In other words, it's only after you meditate on the Word and practice it that you make your way prosperous. Also, notice that this verse does *not* say that God will make your way prosperous.

Many times people misinterpret this verse to read that God will make their way prosperous. Indirectly He does because it's His Word that makes us prosperous, but this verse doesn't say God Himself makes us prosperous. Who makes our way prosperous? Who makes us have good success? We do!

Psalm 1 says the same thing. The person who delights in the Word by meditating on it day and night is the one who prospers: "... *his leaf also shall not wither; and whatsoever he doeth shall prosper*" (Ps. 1:3).

The Amplified Bible says that when you meditate on God's Word, you will be able to deal wisely in the affairs of life. You see, when you make the right decisions and deal wisely in the affairs of life, you begin to prosper. What happens when you make the wrong decisions? In some cases, you won't prosper, and you won't be successful.

I think we've missed the fact that *we* have far more to do with our own prosperity and success than we've ever realized. Yes, it takes faith to be a success. But we've also got to realize that according to these scriptures, another step is also involved. We must meditate on God's Word and practice it. That's how we'll ultimately make our own way prosperous.

Many people know the principles of faith. They know that faith activates the power of God. They know that God wants them to be successful and prosper. Yet many of them haven't succeeded even though they know the Word and are living right! Then what is the problem?

One problem may be found in Joshua 1:8. It says that after you meditate and study the Word, then *you* — not God — will make your own way prosperous. The wisdom of God's Word in you makes you successful. You see, it depends a lot on what *you* do. You've got to fill your heart and mind with the Word so the Word can cause you to deal wisely in all the affairs of life!

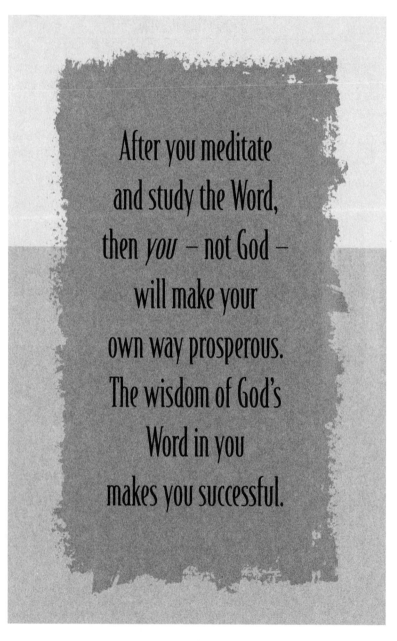

After you meditate
and study the Word,
then *you* – not God –
will make your
own way prosperous.
The wisdom of God's
Word in you
makes you successful.

Sowing and Reaping

"Do not be deceived: God cannot be mocked. A man reaps what he sows. . . .

Let us not become weary in doing good, for at the proper time we will reap a harvest if we do not give up."

— Galatians 6:7,9 (*NIV*)

In the Word of God, you'll find many applications of the principle of seedtime and harvest or sowing and reaping. Usually when people talk about seedtime and harvest, it's in conjunction with giving *money*. But did you know you can sow your entire life into the work of God's Kingdom!

For instance, you can seed your *time* in service to God. When you give God your time, you receive a harvest of blessing in return on your time. You might not be able to figure out how it happens, but when you put God first — fellowshipping with Him and giving of your time for His service — you'll discover that you have more time to do other things!

You can also sow your *talent* to help in the work of the Lord. Your talent may be painting, cleaning, organizing, or something else. But whatever it is, you can get involved in your local church and your community using the talents God gave you to be a blessing to others.

Some people sit around saying, "If I could only do this or that, *then* I'd get involved." No, they wouldn't. If they won't get involved with what they already have to give, then they wouldn't get involved if they had the extra finances, special talents, or whatever else they might think they need.

I like what Peter said to the lame man at the gate called Beautiful. Peter said, "Such as I *have*, give I unto thee" (Acts 3:6). Well, you may not feel you have a lot to offer, but you can be like Peter and decide, "That which I *do* have, I'm going to give!"

Now there's something else you need to know when it comes to seedtime and harvest: you can't just get tired and quit sowing! If you stop sowing, you won't receive your full harvest of reward!

I meet people all the time who have the attitude, *I've worked faithfully in the church, and I've given for years. Now it's my time to sit on the bench.* No, it's never time to sit on the bench.

Sowing and Reaping

It's time to sow more of your time, money, and talents into the work of God than ever before. Paul said, "Don't become weary in well-doing, because you *will* reap a harvest at the proper time *if you don't give up*" (Gal. 6:9)!

Seedtime and harvest is a law that God set into motion, and it works the same way in the spiritual realm as it does in the natural. There is a time to plant, and then there is a time to harvest. You can't expect to sow or plant today and reap an abundant harvest overnight. Why? Because it doesn't work that way. There's a time lapse between the time you sow and the time you reap.

Some time back, the Lord began dealing with me about giving in every offering — whenever an offering bucket goes by — and I teach that to the RHEMA Bible Church congregation. You see, when we continually sow our finances into God's Kingdom, we cut down on the waiting time between harvests. So after a while, money will start coming back on every wave, so to speak, because we're giving on a consistent basis.

You see, friend, you can't out-give God! Whatever you give to God — whether it's your money, your time, or your talents — you can always expect to receive an abundance of blessings in return. So develop a lifestyle of sowing your best into the Kingdom of God, and you'll reap a great harvest of reward all the days of your life!

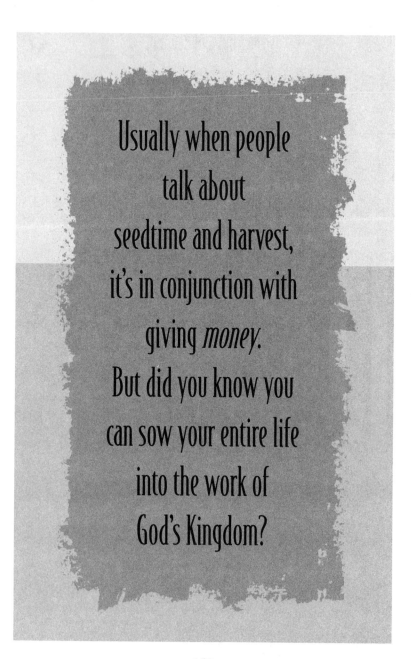

Usually when people
talk about
seedtime and harvest,
it's in conjunction with
giving *money*.
But did you know you
can sow your entire life
into the work of
God's Kingdom?

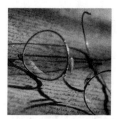

Staying in Shape

FROM A PASTOR'S HEART

Have you ever heard people make these statements: "I've got to get in shape" or "I'm out of shape"? Generally, they're referring to the fact that their physical bodies are not up to par. Maybe they don't fit into the size of clothes they used to wear, or maybe they've simply run out of energy. But basically, they're out of shape! So they make a decision to get back in shape — to begin dieting or to start an exercise program.

Well, it is important to stay in shape physically, but it's also important to stay in shape *spiritually*.

You don't usually hear people talk about being out of shape spiritually, but you don't have to be around some people very long before you realize that they're not up to par spiritually.

However, the good news is that just as we're able to get our bodies back in shape, we're also able to get back in shape spiritually!

It is *our* responsibility to keep ourselves in shape — no one else's! I remember when I was about 17 years old, my track coach once told the team something I never forgot. He said, "It's not my responsibility to keep you in shape; it's *your* responsibility. And it's also your responsibility to be ready to run when it's time to run." What he said really made an impact on me. You see, he was there to give us pointers on running and the strategies on how to run a race. But it wasn't *his* responsibility to keep us in shape — it was *ours*! He wasn't with us 24 hours a day, 7 days a week, to make sure we were keeping ourselves in shape. That responsibility fell on us.

So you're the only one responsible for keeping yourself in shape spiritually. No one else can do it for you. Although there may be several ways to get back into spiritual shape, I'm going to list just a few from the Book of Joshua to help you get started.

Well, one of the best ways is to *absorb* the Word of God on a daily basis — meditate on it day and night (Joshua 1:8). To stay fit naturally, it's important to absorb certain vitamins and minerals into your body to burn as fuel while you're working out. The same principle applies spiritually. Instead of taking in vitamins and minerals, you ingest or absorb the Word of God.

You see, as you live your daily life, you encounter various tests or trials, and you're constantly *giving out* — whether at work, school, home, or wherever you find yourself. So it's important to *take in*. If there's no intake, there can be no outflow. And what you need to intake is the infallible Word of God, which is able to strengthen you and help build you back up.

Another way to stay in shape spiritually is to *cleave* to the Word of God — attach yourself to it, not allowing anything or anyone to cut you loose from it. You also stay in spiritual shape by loving the Lord God with all of your heart, soul, and body (Joshua 23:8,11).

But your spiritual workout is not complete unless you also cultivate a strong attachment to the things of God, such as going to church and assembling yourself together with others of like precious faith. Being in a corporate setting with other believers will give you that extra *oomph* you may need to help you cross over that mountain you're facing.

You see, one of the enemy's greatest tactics is to keep Christians *away* from church, where help is available. For instance, have you ever noticed that sometimes everything under the sun will occur to try and keep you from attending church? Many times when you're going through problems, you're tempted to go the opposite direction and *stay away* from church instead of running *to* church. So you need to cultivate a strong attachment to the things of God.

Now that you know some things you can do to get back in spiritual shape, you can begin right where you are by taking that first step toward your goal.

I remember a story about a 63-year-old woman who *walked* all the way from New York City to Miami, Florida. When she finally reached Miami, she was interviewed by a newspaper reporter. The reporter asked her how she had the courage to make such a long journey on foot. She said, "Oh, it doesn't take courage to take one step at a time!"

Well, just like that woman walked more than one thousand miles by taking one step at a time, it's one step at a time that keeps you spiritually fit. No, you won't become a spiritual giant overnight, but taking one step will get you closer to your goal than where you were yesterday!

Begin today by taking the steps I've mentioned: absorb the Word of God; love the Lord with all that is within you; and go to church to fellowship with those of like precious faith. Staying in shape spiritually *is* obtainable. Why not start today?

One way to stay
in shape spiritually
is to *cleave* to the
Word of God –
attach yourself to it,
not allowing anything
or anyone to cut you
loose from it.

Using Your Talents

The parable of the talents tells the story of a man who divided his fortune among his servants and then traveled to a far country. He gave five talents to one servant, two talents to another, and one talent to another. The servant who had received five talents traded them and gained five more. Likewise, the servant who had received two talents traded them and gained two more. But the servant who had received one talent dug up the earth and hid the talent (Matt. 25:14-30).

The man gave his servants different amounts according to their ability to produce. It's important to note that God knows your ability, and He expects you to produce at that level, not at a part or fraction of your ability.

The local church needs volunteers in every area, and we all have something to contribute. Many believers ask, "How

165

can I get involved?" But most of them don't really want to work in the church. They want the pastor to give them a position — a position means prestige. But it's the people who have been involved and have been faithful that pastors put in leadership positions, because pastors can depend on them to use their talents for God.

Many people have talents, but they're not dependable. For example, they might sign up to volunteer, but they show up when they want to. If something else comes up that they feel is more important than serving as an usher, a nursery worker, or choir member, they do that instead. They think the volunteer job just doesn't amount to anything. Then they wonder why they're not receiving the things they're believing God for. God only rewards those who are faithful.

In the natural, how long do you think you would be employed if you only showed up when you wanted to? Not very long, I assure you. You see, employers reward faithfulness too. Since you're employed to do a job, you receive a paycheck. But if you produce above and beyond your job description, sometimes you get a bonus or a day off with pay as a reward for your faithfulness.

Well, your payday from God might not come after you've been faithful for just two or three weeks. But you will eventually reap rewards for your diligence and faithfulness. And it works that way in every area of life.

Commitment and church involvement are biblical principles that pay rich dividends. Yet in many churches you see the same people volunteering all the time. Do you think they always want to minister to the needs of others? The answer is no. But they're committed to something that is more important than yielding to their flesh. They're committed to serving the Lord.

God doesn't want benchwarmers; He wants people to be involved. Many believers have talents they've never used — they've hidden them.

Other believers cry, "Oh, I want to do something for the Lord." But when you tell them that the local church is full of ministry opportunities, they say, "Oh, that's not what I'm talking about." I've found that people do what they want to do. If they want to get involved, they do. If they don't want to get involved, they always have an excuse.

Did you know that God is not interested in excuses? If you don't believe that, just read about the children of Israel. They came up with all kinds of excuses for why they weren't serving the Lord, but their excuses didn't cut it with God!

You know, some people holler, "Bless me, Lord," but they haven't done anything for Him to bless! The Lord said that He would bless whatever you put your hand to (Deut. 12:7). If you want to receive the blessings of God, then be faithful, committed, and involved.

The parable of the talents shows us that God is not pleased when we don't get involved. But God is highly gratified when we put our talents to work in His Kingdom, and He will reward us!

You have talents that can be used to minister to the Body of Christ, so don't hide them! And if you've buried them, dig them up, and be about your Father's business!

It's the people who have been involved and have been faithful that pastors put in leadership positions, because pastors can depend on them to use their talents for God.

You Want To Be Blessed

"Our barns will be filled with every kind of provision. Our sheep will increase by thousands, by tens of thousands in our fields. . . .

Blessed are the people of whom this is true; BLESSED are the people whose God is the Lord."

— Psalm 144:13,15 *(NIV)*

When you accepted Jesus Christ as your Savior, you were born again and became a child of God. You were translated out of the kingdom of darkness into the Kingdom of God. Your citizenship is now in Heaven, and in Christ you have become a recipient of Heaven's vast resources. As a joint-heir with Jesus Christ and an heir of God, you have become a partaker of all that God possesses. You are a blessed person!

171

God also made a covenant of provision and blessings for His people under the Old Covenant. Once when a Moabite king tried to entice a prophet to curse the Israelites, the prophet responded, *"Behold, I have received commandment to bless: and HE [God] HATH BLESSED; AND I CANNOT REVERSE IT"*(Num. 23:20).

How much more should we be walking in the irreversible blessing of God under the New Covenant, which is a new and better covenant established upon better promises (Heb. 8:6)!

To hear some Christians talk, you would think God is in the business of subtracting blessings *from* people instead of adding blessings *unto* them. But that is not what the Bible teaches.

God *has already blessed* us with all spiritual blessings in Heavenly places and with all things that pertain unto life and godliness (Eph. 1:3; 2 Peter 1:3). But we have our part to play too. We must cooperate with God by studying and meditating upon the Word, and by being doers of the Word in every situation of life, not just when we feel like it.

It will cost you something to walk in the abundant provision and blessings that God promises in His Word. It will take time and diligent effort to make God's Word your top priority.

But it's a small price to pay in order to walk in the fullness of your inheritance in Christ.

When we come in line with God's Word and operate by His principles, we will begin to experience for ourselves the blessings of the inheritance purchased for us by Christ. We will have more than enough, because God is the God who is more than enough, and He will abundantly supply our every need!

Blessed, not *cursed* are the people whose God is the Lord. The inheritance Christ purchased for us at the Cross is a blessing that cannot be reversed.

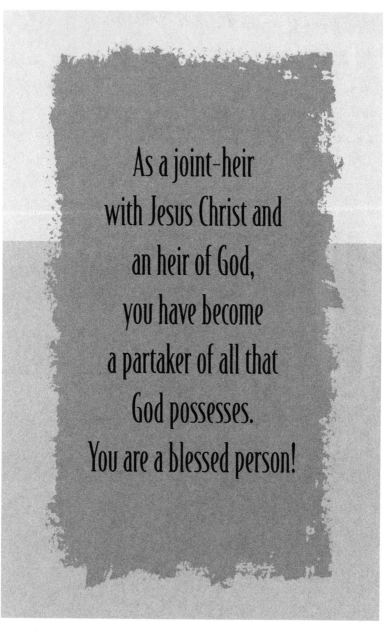

As a joint-heir
with Jesus Christ and
an heir of God,
you have become
a partaker of all that
God possesses.
You are a blessed person!

Your Life Is Interrupted

F R O M   A   P A S T O R ' S   H E A R T

Life's interruptions are those times in life when things just don't seem to go the way we had planned. Interruptions can either make us or break us. We can learn from life's experiences, or we can become resentful and close ourselves off to all that God has for us.

For example, in the Old Testament, Joseph's life was interrupted by some experiences that could have left him bitter and resentful. In each trial that Joseph faced in life, he had a choice to make. He could allow each setback to break him and bring disillusionment or he could allow life's circumstances to make him into the man God desired him to be.

For example, when his brothers sold him into slavery, Joseph could have chosen to be bitter. And when he was thrown into prison, Joseph again could have become resentful and angry. After all, people had failed Joseph! His own brothers sold him into slavery, Pharaoh's wife lied about him, and the cup-bearer forgot about him. Joseph had every opportunity to lose faith, not only in people, but also in his dreams!

However, if Joseph had become bitter, he never would have achieved in life what God had already designed and purposed for him.

You see, each of us can use life's interruptions to make us or break us. We can use these experiences for the glory of God by allowing them to mold us into the people God needs us to be to complete His work on this earth.

For example, life's interruptions can teach us how to handle our pride. Many times life doesn't go quite like we think it should because we think more highly of ourselves than we ought. But if we'll allow God to teach us in the situations of life instead of just griping and complaining, we will grow spiritually and profit by life's experiences. And if we will allow them to, life's interruptions can prepare us for greater service for God.

When life doesn't go just exactly as you think it should, instead of getting negative and downcast, look for the light of God at the end of the tunnel. When interruptions come along, and you're feeling overwhelmed, say, "Father, please use this situation to prepare me for greater service for You."

Life's interruptions not only prepared Joseph for greater service, but these interruptions — the pit, Potiphar, and the prison — also equipped him to assist Pharaoh, the ruler of Egypt (*See* Genesis chapters 37-45).

Life's interruptions caused Joseph to be in a position where doors opened to him that never would have opened otherwise. Pharaoh said to Joseph, "See, I have set thee over all the land of Egypt" (Gen. 41:41). In other words, Pharaoh placed Joseph in a unique position of authority. Joseph had been well-prepared by God to succeed!

I'm sure that when Joseph was thrown into that pit as a boy and sold as a slave, he wondered how his dreams were ever going to come true. When he sat in that prison cell, Joseph may have questioned God, "How can this be possible? I know what You showed me!"

But God turned every one of life's interruptions to Joseph's benefit as he trusted God and did not allow his heart to become bitter and resentful. Because Joseph kept his heart right before God and allowed Him to work in his life, God brought Joseph from the pit to the position of prime minister of Egypt! Joseph came to a place of great prominence and success in life because he put his faith in God and refused to allow any interruptions to keep him down!

177

Joseph allowed life's experiences to teach him humility and to show him that God can work in any situation. Also, Joseph let these interruptions teach him that God's opportunities would remain available to him as long as he stayed obedient to God!

When you are confronted with life's interruptions, stay in faith and declare, "My situation may be impossible with man, but it is possible with God" (Luke 18:27). Then allow God to turn that impossible situation in your life to your good and to His glory!

When life doesn't go just
exactly as you think it
should, instead of getting
negative and downcast,
look for the light of God
at the end of the tunnel.

INSPIRED WORDS

CONCERNING

Peace

FOR THE SEASONS

OF YOUR LIFE

Building a Strong Foundation

F R O M   A   P A S T O R ' S   H E A R T

"Therefore whosoever heareth these sayings of mine, and doeth them, I [Jesus] will liken him unto a wise man, which built his house upon a rock:

And the rain descended, and the floods came, and the winds blew, and beat upon that house; and it fell not: FOR IT WAS FOUNDED UPON A ROCK."

— Matthew 7:24,25

If you've ever studied about eagles, you know that these magnificent birds build their nests high upon mountaintops in the cleft of a rock, thousands of feet above the valley floor. The eagle's nest is unique because it is built with logs and branches — some of them weighing as much as the eagle itself!

After the eagle secures its nest with large branches, it uses smaller branches, twigs, and soft down feathers to pad the nest. An eagle's nest is built to last and can withstand high winds of more than one hundred miles an hour.

We need to take a lesson from the eagle and build our spiritual dwelling place high within the cleft of a rock! That Rock is the Lord Jesus Christ and His eternal Word. When our lives are built on the firm foundation of the Rock of Ages, we will be strong and secure in every test and trial of life.

In fact, if you are going to fulfill what God wants for your life, you *must* build on the foundation of His Word. Your life will not make sense until you build your life on Jesus Christ, the Rock.

Protected by His sheltering arms, Jesus will keep you safe from the storms of life. And a relationship with Jesus is stronger than any eagle's nest — it is a dwelling place for eternity! When you are dwelling safe and secure with Jesus, the winds and storms of this life will not be able to shake your strong foundation.

In the very midst of the storm, the eagle snuggles down into its nest, safe from harm, because that nest was built properly. When you base your life on God's Word, you can snuggle down safe and secure in your spiritual dwelling place in Christ.

Building a Strong Foundation

And you can withstand any test or trial because your life is built upon the rock of the Word.

The devil can howl all he wants to, but the circumstances and storms of life cannot defeat you! Peace and strength come from dwelling in the shelter of God's Word. You need not tremble and shake in life's storms when your life is built securely on God's Word.

You see, some Christians do not take time to build their lives properly founded on the Word. When the enemy hits them with a trial, they try to construct a secure dwelling place in the midst of the storm.

But laying a firm foundation in the midst of a storm is no fun! And when the enemy comes against you, you don't have time to get involved in a construction project!

So build your foundation strong and secure on the Word in the first place. Learn a valuable lesson from the eagle and build your foundation upon the sure rock — the Lord Jesus Christ and His Word!

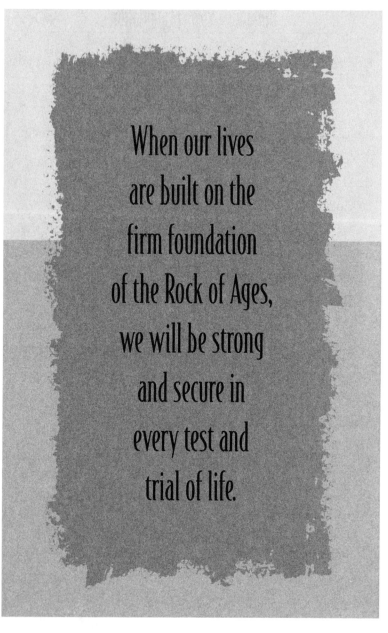

When our lives
are built on the
firm foundation
of the Rock of Ages,
we will be strong
and secure in
every test and
trial of life.

Leaning on God's Everlasting Arms

"THE ETERNAL GOD IS THY REFUGE, *and UNDERNEATH ARE THE EVERLASTING ARMS: and he shall thrust out the enemy from before thee; and shall say, Destroy them.*"

— Deuteronomy 33:27

A refuge is a shelter or a place of protection from danger or distress. It's a safe place. God's everlasting arms are a safe place and a refuge for every one of us to run into for protection and safety.

God's everlasting arms are arms of power and strength. Jeremiah 32:17 says, *"Ah Lord God! behold, thou hast made the heaven and the earth by thy great power and STRETCHED OUT ARM, and there is nothing too hard for thee."*

187

Nothing is too hard for the God who made Heaven and earth by His great power and His outstretched, everlasting arms! Commenting on this verse, one writer said, "The Lord stretched out His arms and opened His hand and flung the worlds into existence."

God created the universe with His mighty power! If God can create the universe with His mighty power, He can create whatever it is you need in your life. There's nothing in your life that's too hard for Him! Just lean on His everlasting arms!

The Word of God says that He is the Lord; He changes not, and He's not a man that He should lie (Num. 23:19). Therefore, since God has not changed, He still has the mighty power in His outstretched arms that He's always had. What do you need in your life? Look to your Refuge — God Almighty. His powerful, outstretched arms are not lacking in strength or ability to help you!

God's power is still available to you today. God wants to stretch out His mighty arms on your behalf. The Bible says, "He hath shewed strength with his arm . . ." (Luke 1:51). Do you need God's strength shown in your life today?

Look to Him! Seek Him with all your heart. God says in His Word, "Am I a God at hand, saith the Lord, and not a God afar off?" (Jer. 23:23). His ear is open to the cry of the righteous, and He longs to demonstrate His power to you. The Bible says to *"Trust in him at all times; ye people, pour out your heart before him: God is a refuge for us"* (Ps. 62:8). Run into the refuge of His everlasting arms and find the answers you need.

Allow God to be your refuge. Look to Him and to the power in His Word. Lean on His everlasting arms. He will not fail you. As you seek Him with all your heart, He will stretch out His mighty, powerful arms to bring you to a place of safety and peace.

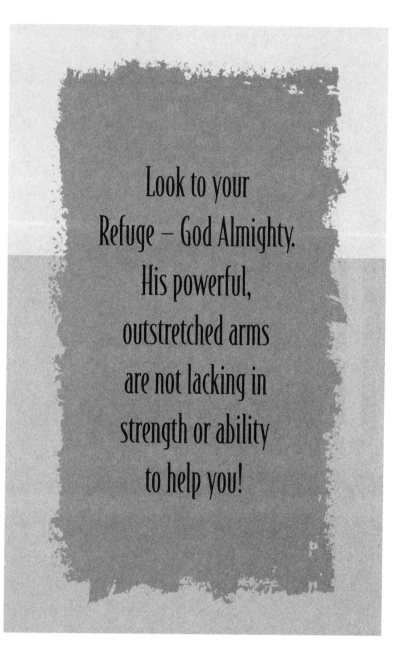

Look to your
Refuge – God Almighty.
His powerful,
outstretched arms
are not lacking in
strength or ability
to help you!

Needing Rest

"*Come unto me, all ye that labour and are heavy laden, and I will give you rest.*"

— Matthew 11:28

Sometimes we don't understand the full context of certain scriptures, because the Bible reflects the times and customs of people from an Eastern culture. But try to picture for a moment the world in which Jesus lived.

Donkeys and camels loaded down with heavy cargo travelled along the dusty roads. Women and young children often walked the streets like beasts themselves, balancing across their shoulders yokes on which clay pots or various wares were hung. In every town and village, you could find beggars who were deaf, blind, or lame. And everywhere you looked, you saw poor and oppressed people whose burdens in life were great. This is the world to whom Jesus first said, "Come unto Me. Take My yoke; it's easy."

Well, things are not much different in our society today. Of course, in most parts of the Western world, you won't see folks carrying literal yokes. And there might not be as many who beg in public streets. Yet people are *spiritually* impaired, and they're walking around laden with all sorts of burdens.

But even though the world today is still full of oppression, rejection, disappointment, and uncertainties, Jesus is still saying, "Come unto Me!"

You may say, "But I've already come to Jesus. I'm a born-again believer." Yes, you may have come to God for salvation, but you can continue to come to Him for grace, strength, rest, and encouragement.

You see, it's possible — even as a believer — to become burdened and weighted down as you walk through life. For example, you may not walk in love as you ought, and it may cause your faith to become weakened. Or you might experience some inconsistencies in your relationship with the Lord. Well, Jesus is saying, "Come unto Me, you who labor but sometimes find yourself not living for Me as consistently as you should be"!

Needing Rest

God's promise of divine relief and rest is for anyone who'll accept it. It doesn't matter who you are or what you're facing.

Are you troubled and ill-at-ease? Are the pressures of life weighing you down? Do you need relief from the stress and strain of your present situation? Could you use some rest for your soul?

If so, Jesus says, "Come unto Me. Come hear My voice. Come into My Presence, and experience My grace and strength." He's extending the invitation to you, but He won't force you to accept it. *You're* going to have to do something; you're going to have to "come unto Him"!

You're also going to have to be willing to exchange your yoke for His yoke. Jesus said, *"Take my yoke upon you, and learn of me; for I am meek and lowly in heart: and ye shall find rest unto your souls"* (Matt. 11:29).

In other words, when you come to the Lord, you'll have to submit yourself to His guidance and authority and obey what He says to do. You're saved by *faith*, but you enter into God's rest by *obedience*!

Aren't you glad that God provided a way of escape from the pressures of life? Aren't you glad that He's not off somewhere in the distance, leaving you to deal with your own affairs the best you know how?

You can draw strength and encouragement from the Lord's invitation for whatever you need today. Jesus Christ, the Anointed One, can remove any burden and destroy any yoke in your life. And He is saying to *you*, "I am your Deliverer! Come unto Me. I will give you rest!"

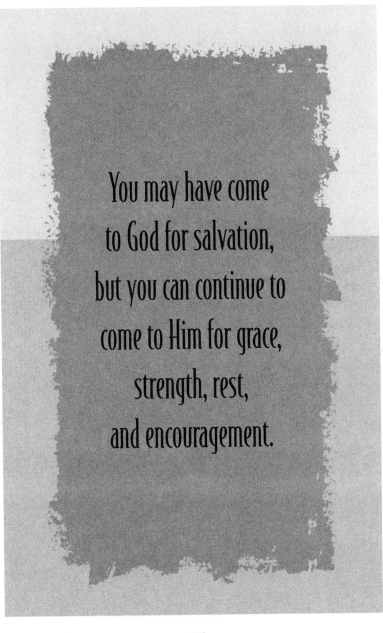

You may have come
to God for salvation,
but you can continue to
come to Him for grace,
strength, rest,
and encouragement.

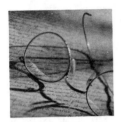

Needing Safety and Peace

"The Lord is my light and my salvation — whom shall I fear? The Lord is the stronghold of my life — of whom shall I be afraid? . . .

For in the day of trouble he will keep me safe in his dwelling; he will hide me in the shelter of his tabernacle and set me high upon a rock."

— Psalm 27:1,5 (*NIV*)

The Lord is the stronghold of our lives. That means He is our strength and stability, our ever-present help in times of trouble (Ps. 46:1). He is our safe haven, our strong tower, and our fortress. He provides us with security, peace, and comfort. We can continually run to Him for protection from all harm.

Our God is a mighty fortress! He's a never-failing bulwark or support for us in times of trouble in life. The word "bulwark" is defined as a *solid wall-like structure raised for defense*. The Lord will defend us in the storms of life; He is also our defense against the enemy. In everything we do for His glory, God strengthens us for the task with His mighty power.

When you make God your stronghold in life, you will not waver in faith like you're on a spiritual roller coaster. No matter what happens or what *doesn't* happen, you can remain stable and immovable — protected because you abide in the secret place of the most High, "under the shadow of the Almighty" (Ps. 91:1).

When God is your strength and stronghold in life, nothing can affect you. Even when the devil tries to attack you, or when circumstances change, or when things don't go like you think they should, you can stand strong knowing that nothing can shake you from God's firm and loving hold on your life.

We can always rest safe and secure by staying in God's stronghold of protection! What is God's stronghold of protection? It's found in His Word. It's found by dwelling in His Presence.

When you dwell in God's Presence, fortified with His Word, you gain courage and confidence in your God. You know He's faithful to take care of you in every situation.

Psalm 27:5 says, *"For in the time of trouble he shall hide me in his pavilion: in the secret of his tabernacle shall he hide me; he shall set me up upon a rock."*

The Bible says that in times of trouble, God will set us high upon a rock. Who is the Rock? His Name is Jesus! When God sets us high above circumstances on Jesus, the Rock of Ages, nothing can touch us because He is our protection.

The Bible also says that in times of trouble, God will hide us in His tabernacle or pavilion. What does that mean? Because we're saved, God dwells in us and we dwell in Him. We live and move and have our being in God (Acts 17:28). God dwells in our tabernacle, our being, and we dwell in Him.

Have you made God the stronghold of your life? Make Him your strong tower, so He can fortify and strengthen your life. Then you will dwell in safety and peace.

When you dwell in
God's Presence,
fortified with His Word,
you gain courage and
confidence in your God.
You know He's faithful
to take care of you
in every situation.

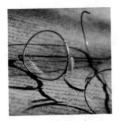

Overburdened With the Cares of Life

"Casting the whole of your care [all your anxieties, all your worries, all your concerns, once and for all] on Him, for He cares for you affectionately and cares about you watchfully."

— 1 Peter 5:7 (*Amplified*)

Have you ever asked yourself the questions, *Does God really care about me? Does He know what I'm going through?*

I'm sure at one time or another all of us have felt like no one cared about us and the problems we were facing in life. Maybe there's even been a time when we thought God Himself didn't care.

But God does care about us. Psalm 55:22 says, *"Cast thy burden upon the Lord, and he shall sustain thee: he shall never suffer the righteous to be moved."*

In other words, we can cast our cares on God, and He will sustain us because we are in right standing with Him. If we will just commit our burdens to Him and keep walking with Him, His Word promises us that we cannot fail.

Of course, the enemy wants us to think about all of our problems and try to work them out ourselves. But once we begin to carry our own burdens, then we've really got problems! Problems and difficulties may come, but we've got to learn how to cast them over on God so *He* can work them out!

There is a secret to living a peaceful life of happiness in the Lord. And it is to cast all of our problems, burdens, griefs, and anxieties on the Lord! I didn't say that would always be easy to do. It is probably one of the hardest things to do because problems have a way of grabbing our attention, and we want to try to figure them out.

We will all face problems and trials in life. Sometimes we face circumstances that can overwhelm us if we don't look to the Word of God and keep our eyes on Him. The feelings we experience are real, but God and His Word are bigger than our feelings or any problem! God did not create us and then just leave us to take care of ourselves — He cares about us!

Have you ever noticed that when you're feeling down and depressed, it's usually because *you* are carrying all the cares, worries, and anxieties of life upon your own shoulders?

God knew you would have burdens and anxieties in this life. And God said in His Word to *cast*, *throw*, or *commit* your burdens on Him! *You* do not have to carry your own burdens. There is One who carried them for you, and His Name is Jesus. He can work out everything you commit to Him because He cares!

There is a
secret to living
a peaceful life of
happiness in the Lord.
And it is to
cast all of our problems,
burdens, griefs, and
anxieties on the Lord!

Reflecting on the Goodness of God

"For out of His fullness (abundance) we have all received [all had a share and we were all supplied with] one grace after another and spiritual blessing upon spiritual blessing, and even favor upon favor and gift [heaped] upon gift."

— John 1:16 (*Amplified*)

We need to reflect on the goodness of God. The Bible says that God has heaped upon us spiritual blessing upon spiritual blessing, favor upon favor, and gift upon gift.

Another translation says, "From the fullness of His grace, we have all received one blessing after another." The goodness of God is far greater than you and I can even think or imagine!

205

We are all aware that in ourselves we do not deserve the blessings of God. In ourselves we are nothing, but in Christ, each one of us is precious and valuable to God. And it is only by the grace of God that we are privileged to have a relationship with our Heavenly Father through our Lord Jesus Christ.

We sing about the marvelous grace of our loving Lord, grace that is greater than all our sins. We can never do anything to merit the grace of God, and we can never be good enough to receive it. But God in His own mercy freely extends His bountiful grace to us and has blessed us with all spiritual blessings in Christ Jesus.

Think about how great the grace of God really is! We do not have to stand before God on our own merit. By the blood of the Lord Jesus Christ, we can come boldly before God without fear or trembling. Because of Jesus, God is our own Heavenly Father.

The source of all our blessings flows from the Lord Jesus Christ. It is because of the Gift that God gave to mankind — the Lord Jesus Christ — that we have received blessing after blessing and favor upon favor.

We have received these bountiful treasures from a heavenly Source — our Lord Jesus Christ. These spiritual gifts come from the very heart of God. God sent Jesus that we might have life. He did not have to send Jesus to this earth to redeem us, but He did.

Think about it! Jesus chose to accept the death on the Cross for us. He didn't have to, but He chose to do it for you and me. We need to understand that all of our blessings, all of our joy, and every good thing we have today is a result of what Jesus did for us when He gave the greatest gift of all — His life for the redemption of mankind.

Let us reflect on God's goodness to us. And let's especially take time to thank God for His greatest gift to mankind — our precious Heavenly Gift — the Lord Jesus Christ and the salvation He so freely provided for us!

We need to understand
that all of our blessings,
all of our joy, and every
good thing we have today
is a result of what Jesus
did for us when He gave
the greatest gift of all –
His life for the
redemption of mankind.

You Are Insecure

Over the years I've had the chance to travel quite a bit and to talk to many different people. And I've discovered that there are a lot of insecure folks — even Christians — in the world today. But of all people, *Christians* should be the ones who are the most confident and established.

I like what David said in Psalm 26:1 and 2. He said, ". . . I have trusted in the Lord without wavering. Test me, O Lord, and try me, examine my heart and my mind" (*NIV*).

That's a pretty strong claim. As a rule, if you're not really up to par, you don't want anyone to examine you too closely, let alone God. But David invited God to explore his claims. He said, "Here I am. Examine me!"

Now some people boast about themselves simply because way down, deep inside, they're really insecure. They feel inadequate. So they try to compensate by being very vocal. And most of the time, they're not telling the truth.

But I want you to notice that Psalm 26:1 and 2 aren't the boastful words of a weak, insecure man. They're the statements of a person who is genuinely secure in who he is and what he is! Notice that David's security wasn't in and of *himself*; his security was in the Lord! David wasn't boasting in himself; he was boasting in the Lord. He said, ". . . I have trusted *in the Lord* without wavering. . . . I walk continually *in your truth*" (vv. 1,3 *NIV*).

That's a real key that you and I can pick up on: To walk in the way of truth is to walk in *security*; but to walk in the way of wavering is to walk in *insecurity*.

In other words, you've got to come to the place in trusting God that you determine, "No matter what I get hit with in life, I'm going to scramble back to my feet. And no matter what happens, I'm not going to waver from the truth of God's Word!"

You see, it's the insecure and defeated who *stay* down when they get knocked off their feet. But the secure get back up and keep going because they know that as long as they stay in the fight, they're going to win!

You might say, "Yeah, but you don't know what I've been going through. You don't know all the trials and tribulations I've been facing."

No, but the Word says that if you'll trust God, you won't be moved or shaken. If you'll put all your trust in Him, you can take refuge under the shadow of His wings until every calamity has passed (Ps. 21:7; 57:1)!

Friend, you do *not* have to be like others who are wavering, unsure of who they are and what they're doing. That's what the devil wants you to believe so he can keep you feeling inept and insecure. But when he comes to you with those lies, don't whine and whimper and go around making excuses. Just stand your ground, and tell the devil to flee in Jesus' Name.

Then lift up your voice and start praising the Lord — because you know where your security lies. You're trusting in the Word of God, the eternal Rock. And there is absolutely no greater security than that!

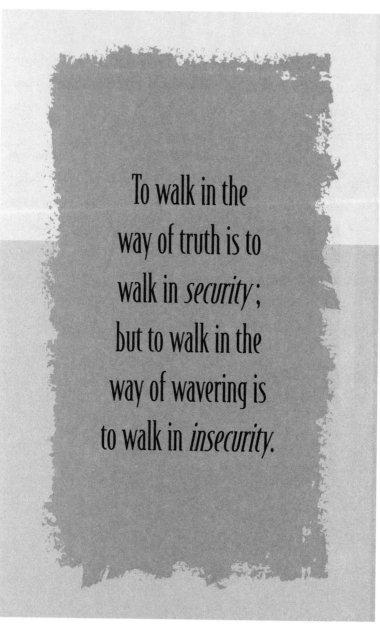

To walk in the
way of truth is to
walk in *security*;
but to walk in the
way of wavering is
to walk in *insecurity*.

You Desire a Loyal Friend

A *"And it came to pass . . . that the soul of Jonathan was knit with the soul of David, and Jonathan loved him as his own soul. . . . Then Jonathan and David made a covenant, because he loved him as his own soul."*

— 1 Samuel 18:1,3

What a wonderful example of a friend's love and loyalty! Jonathan's own father, King Saul, was trying to kill David who had been anointed to take Saul's place as King of Israel. But Jonathan remained devoted to his friend, David, even though it meant giving up his own legal right to his father's throne. Jonathan's friendship and undying loyalty to David saved David's life and prepared the way for him to take his rightful place as God's chosen king for God's people.

213

Too many people in the world today know little about the kind of steadfast loyalty and love Jonathan showed to his beloved friend, David. They know even less about the unconditional love of God — the kind of love that abides and endures through changing times and the stormy winds of adversity and uncertainty.

People everywhere long for relationships motivated by such a love. And in the midst of the chaos and unpredictability of the world today, God has made a way through Jesus Christ for each of us to have that kind of a relationship *with God Himself!*

Jesus said, *"Greater love hath no man than this, that a man lay down his life for his friends"* (John 15:13). Jesus initiated the greatest friendship man could ever know when He willingly came to the earth and laid down His life to redeem every person from sin and from the clutches of Satan. Jesus' act of unconditional love proved once and for all His commitment to befriend man.

The Bible says Jesus is the Friend who sticks closer than a brother (Prov. 18:24) and that in Christ, nothing can separate us from His great love (Rom. 8:39). There is no safer place to find a refuge of peace, rest, and tranquility in the midst of life's storms than with Jesus, your Beloved Friend.

You can begin this relationship with Jesus Christ by accepting Him as your Savior and Lord. And you can continually enjoy communion and fellowship with Him by desiring His matchless companionship and by drawing near to Him through His Word.

To know Jesus better is to trust Him more. The more you know about Jesus and His love for you, the more you will come to rely on His faithfulness and embrace Him as your Beloved Friend.

Jesus initiated the greatest friendship man could ever know when He willingly came to the earth and laid down His life to redeem every person from sin and from the clutches of Satan.

You Want To Be Free

You and I are free today from the chains of sin, sickness, and disease because Jesus Christ became our Substitute upon the Cross of Calvary (Isa. 53). Jesus paid a price we could not pay.

There is nothing you or I could have done to gain our citizenship in Heaven. Our citizenship in Heaven was bought and paid for by Jesus Christ. It took Jesus' shed blood to buy our redemption.

The Cross of Calvary is real. It is not a myth or a fairy tale. Jesus shed His blood for our redemption when He hung upon that Cross so many years ago. And now the Cross is both a warning to those who refuse to believe and a blessing to those who recognize that it stands for the grace of God.

We do not merit God's favor and grace. All of God's blessings were bought and paid for when Jesus became our Substitute upon the Cross of Calvary. God's grace and mercy are now ours to freely receive.

If it were not for the Cross and Jesus' shed blood, we would have received justice. We would have had to pay the price for our own sins — something we could never do. But instead of receiving justice, we have received abundant mercy and grace because Jesus paid the price for us!

In our judicial system, sometimes the judge has the ability to be lenient and show mercy, or if need be, he can penalize an offender to the full limits of the law. Many times offenders will throw themselves on the mercy of the court, hoping to receive mercy instead of judgment. I thank God that the Judge of all the earth, God Almighty, has given unlimited mercy to those who come to the Cross — the symbol of Jesus' redemption to all of mankind.

The Judge of all the earth has already extended mercy to you. Because of Jesus, all you have to do is accept His mercy. When you know Jesus and you are born again, you can stand before God fresh and clean because of the Cross of Calvary.

You see, because of Jesus' death on the Cross, we have passed from death to life (1 John 3:14). And every Christian has the hope that when he leaves this life, he goes to be with Jesus in Heaven and to begin his life there.

Because Jesus chose to become the Supreme Sacrifice for our sins and to die and shed His blood, you and I have life and have it more abundantly (John 10:10). This is the greatest story ever told to mankind. Someone — God's own Son — has taken our place and paid our debt of sin. And now we are free!

Because Jesus chose
to become the
Supreme Sacrifice
for our sins and to die
and shed His blood,
you and I have life
and have it
more abundantly.

INSPIRED WORDS

CONCERNING

Revival

FOR THE SEASONS

OF YOUR LIFE

Desiring More of God's Glory

FROM A PASTOR'S HEART

"The Spirit of the Lord is upon me, because he hath anointed me to preach the gospel to the poor; he hath sent me to heal the brokenhearted, to preach deliverance to the captives, and recovering of sight to the blind, to set at liberty them that are bruised, To preach the acceptable year of the Lord."

— Luke 4:18,19

You and I as believers have a responsibility to take the reality of God's power to those who are in need. All the anointing and power we will ever need to produce a mighty revival throughout this earth is available to the Body of Christ *right now*. I believe we are standing on the brink of a great move of God and a mighty outpouring of His Spirit.

I was just a child when the great healing revivals began in the 1940s. Those revivals didn't come because people just sat around, saying, "Revival is coming! Revival is coming!" No, those revivals came because men and women of God set their faces like flint toward the Lord and sought Him with all of their hearts.

God's glory is revealed when men and women *seek* God's glory and *prepare* themselves before Him to be channels of His glory to bless mankind. And as my dad, Rev. Kenneth E. Hagin, has said many times, preparation time is never wasted time.

I remember as a child how Dad would spend hours on end in prayer, seeking God because he sensed there was something more to come in the move of God upon the earth. Dad never prayed for the Lord to use him or to put him at the forefront of the next wave of revival. But he did pray, "Lord, make me a blessing wherever I go." Dad hungered with all of his being for the glory of God to be revealed and the plan of God to be consummated on the earth.

Many in the Body of Christ have the mistaken idea that God has only chosen certain ministers to seek His face and to be vessels of His glory and power in the earth today. But God is beckoning *all believers* everywhere to draw near to Him and become men and women of destiny in this hour, fulfilling God's plan in the earth.

So don't leave "seeking God" for someone else to do. The Bible says, *"The glory of this latter house shall be greater than of the former . . ."* (Hag. 2:9). Great men and women of God from yesteryear have lived and died, having blazed a trail before us. They tasted some of the glory which is yet to be revealed to us, and they were faithful to pass on the vision — the torch of revival which burned so deeply in their hearts.

Who will dare to pay the price to take the reality of God's power and glory to those in need? Revival comes when there is revival in men's and women's *hearts*. So let us run the race and finish the course that God has set before us. We need to diligently seek God's face, keeping the torch lit and the flame of revival burning brightly in our hearts.

And we need to direct man's eyes to Jesus, not to a minister or a manifestation. It's as we lift up and exalt Jesus that men will be drawn unto Him (John 12:32). And the Spirit of the Lord will be upon the Body of Christ like never before to preach the Gospel, heal the sick, and set the captives free — and God's glory will be revealed in all the earth!

God is beckoning
all believers
everywhere to draw
near to Him and become
men and women
of destiny in this hour,
fulfilling God's plan
in the earth.

Filling the Earth With the Knowledge of God

"For the earth shall be filled with the knowledge of the glory of the Lord, as the waters cover the sea."

— Habakkuk 2:14

We frequently hear the term "the knowledge of the Lord." According to Colossians 1:9 and 10, God desires that we be filled with the knowledge of Him and His will. When the knowledge of the Lord fills the land, the Spirit of God will manifest Himself mightily!

The Word of God tells us that God has chosen to dwell in human vessels. So the human vessels He has chosen to indwell need to be filled with the knowledge of God before the knowledge of God can fill the earth!

You as a believer need to have a personal knowledge of God. You shouldn't just let someone stand behind a pulpit and tell you about God without your getting involved in knowing God *for yourself*. With your own eyes, read the Word and devour it. Find out for yourself what God's Word has to say about your life in Christ.

The Gospel of the Lord Jesus Christ is simple. Man's theology and religion have tried to make it difficult. But in Jesus' earthly ministry, He always kept His teaching very simple. And yet in His simplicity, Jesus was very profound.

Man's theology did not bring you into a personal relationship with God. The *Word of God* brought you into a personal knowledge of Him. And through the knowledge of God and His Word, you can maintain a lifestyle of victory and success because you know the Victor and the Conqueror — *Jesus!* Because of Him, you have become more than a conqueror (Rom. 8:37).

Part of knowing God is meditating in His Word and putting it into operation in your everyday life. For example, you can know the keys on a musical keyboard. But until you actually begin to play those keys, no music will come forth. It's operating in the knowledge you have that produces results.

We as the Body of Christ need to get ahold of the knowledge of God as we devour the pages of God's Word for ourselves. Then we can each operate in our place filled with the knowledge of God. As we do, the whole earth will be filled with the knowledge of God, and mighty demonstrations of His power and glory will come upon the earth!

The Word of God tells us
that God has chosen to
dwell in human vessels.
So the human vessels He
has chosen to indwell need
to be filled with the
knowledge of God before
the knowledge of God
can fill the earth!

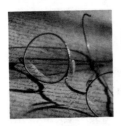

Guarding Your Heart

"According as his divine power hath given unto us ALL THINGS THAT PERTAIN UNTO LIFE AND GODLINESS . . .

Whereby are given unto us exceeding great and precious promises: that by these ye might be partakers of the divine nature, having escaped the corruption that is in the world through lust."

— 2 Peter 1:3,4

I want to stir up your mind to remind you that you have been given all things that pertain to life and godliness. But it is up to you to guard what God has given you.

I see many in the Body of Christ today who are moving on with God and staying with what God has told them to do. But I also see those who are moving in another direction.

231

They're leaning to the arm of flesh and following after man's programs. Some have become so involved with promoting the newest evangelism program or the latest doctrine that they've lost sight of what God has given *them* to do. They've even begun to compromise the basics of faith that have brought them up to this point.

A similar problem must have existed in Jeremiah's day because he said, ". . . *Cursed be the man that trusteth in man, and maketh flesh his arm, and whose heart departeth from the Lord*" (Jer. 17:5).

The Bible says that in the last days people will have "itching ears," heaping unto themselves teachers who will teach them what they want to hear (2 Tim. 4:3). So be on your guard. Don't get caught up in new doctrines and programs that rob you of the truth of God's Word.

You can't afford to become entangled with something that sounds and looks good but denies the power of God. You have to stand firm upon your convictions of faith and what you believe concerning the Word of God, no matter who comes down the road teaching something to the contrary.

Friend, we can't allow the enemy to turn us aside from the things that God has so freely given us. We've come too far to be robbed of the blessings that still lie within reach. We've come this far by faith; now is no time to quit!

The enemy is doing everything he can to try to stop the Church of the Lord Jesus Christ. He is coming forth in full battle array because he knows that his time is short. But the devil hasn't been able to stop the move of the power of God since it was poured out upon the Church on the Day of Pentecost!

And now in this hour, faith and the anointing of the Spirit of God are in *our* hearts. But it's up to *us* to guard those treasures!

I believe that the Church is on the brink of a major revival. People are being saved by the blood of the Lord Jesus Christ, healed, filled with the Holy Spirit, and set free from the chains of the enemy as never before. And you and I have a part to play in this mighty move of God.

I want to encourage you not to let anything or anyone stop you from doing what God has called you to do. Stay with the Word and the anointing of the Spirit of God. It's the truth of God's Word and the power of His Spirit that will give you a "backbone of steel"; they'll give you the strength to face any danger and to minister to a lost, hurting world.

Make every effort in the days to come to guard your heart as tenaciously as a bulldog guards his favorite bone. Take your stand in the power of the Spirit and in the word of faith, and don't back down from the truth that God has given you!

You have to stand firm
upon your convictions
of faith and what
you believe concerning
the Word of God,
no matter who comes
down the road
teaching something
to the contrary.

Ushering in the Power of God

F R O M   A   P A S T O R ' S   H E A R T

". . . They lifted up their voice to God with ONE ACCORD, and said, Lord, thou art God, which hast made heaven, and earth, and the sea, and all that in them is. . . .

And when they had prayed, THE PLACE WAS SHAKEN where they were assembled together . . . ."

— Acts 4:24,31

I want you to notice that when the disciples were gathered together in one accord, they lifted their voices unto God with singleness of purpose. When they came together in that kind of unity, the house where they were gathered literally shook like a leaf in the wind.

We believers need to realize that when we as the Body of Christ begin to unite ourselves together in the unity and the

235

power of the Word of God, we are going to see some places shaken by the power of God that have never been shaken before.

You see, one reason God has been hindered from demonstrating His power in the fullness He desires is that believers have only united themselves together *at times* in unity and harmony.

The word "unity" carries with it the meaning of one mind, one aim, and one purpose. What is our mind, aim, and purpose to be centered around? It is to glorify God and to lift up Jesus Christ, because Jesus said, "If I be lifted up, I will draw all men unto Me" (John 12:32).

Unity comes as we forget about our different personalities and unite ourselves around the Word of God. As we do, we will see ourselves ushered into an age of God's power such as you and I have never seen.

The Word of God says, "Greater works shall you do because I go to My Father" (John 14:12). We have yet to see the greater works accomplished because we, the Church of the Lord Jesus Christ, have failed to unite ourselves as we should have. As a result, God has been hindered from moving as He desires.

I believe when the Body of Christ is in unity, every gift of the Spirit will be in operation, and every fruit of the spirit will be developed in our lives. Then and only then can the power of God be demonstrated fully.

In this last day before Jesus Christ Himself comes and splits the clouds of glory, I believe the Body of Christ will come together in one mind, one aim, and one purpose. Then we will see the power of Almighty God in demonstration as we have never seen it before!

Unity comes as we
forget about our different
personalities and unite
ourselves around the
Word of God.
As we do, we will see
ourselves ushered into an
age of God's power such as
you and I have never seen.

You Need Understanding Of the Word

"The eyes of your understanding being enlightened; that ye may know what is THE HOPE OF HIS CALLING, and what is THE RICHES OF THE GLORY OF HIS INHERITANCE IN THE SAINTS,

And what is THE EXCEEDING GREATNESS OF HIS POWER TO USWARD WHO BELIEVE, according to the working of his mighty power."

— Ephesians 1:18,19

In the natural, if you are blind and can't see, it doesn't matter how bright and beautiful the scenery is, you won't be able to see it. Or, for example, what good is the beauty of a diamond if you can't behold it?

But did you know that the same thing is true when it comes to seeing the things of God? All the wonders and treasures of God can be found in the pages of God's Word. But if the eyes of your understanding aren't enlightened or opened to the truth of the Word, you won't see God's hidden riches.

You see, it's with the heart that Christians see spiritual things in the first place. In other words, in order to really understand the Word of God, we need to understand in our heart or spirit what our inheritance is in Christ.

In fact, many times spiritual things don't make sense to our natural, carnal mind. We understand the truth of God's Word first in our spirit and then it comes into our mind.

Therefore, you need to look with your heart at what God says in His Word. Quit trying to figure the Bible out with your head! Ask God to open the eyes of your understanding so you can understand the spiritual riches that He's provided just for *you*, His child!

God wants the eyes of our understanding opened! He wants us to see or perceive the wonders of our inheritance in Christ! Actually, there are three things about our inheritance in Christ that God wants us to be able to perceive with our heart.

First, He wants us to know *the hope of His call on our lives*. Second, God wants us to know *the glorious riches of His inheritance* to us, His saints. And third, God wants us to know *the exceeding greatness of His power* working on behalf of those of us who believe Him.

How do we get the eyes of our understanding enlightened to see the riches that God has provided for us? For one thing, we can pray these prayers to God for ourselves. The Bible says that the Word of God never returns void. It always accomplishes what it was sent to do (Isa. 55:11).

Then as we stay in God's Presence and in His Word, the eyes of our understanding will begin to be enlightened so we can receive the knowledge of His will in every area of our lives. Once our eyes are opened spiritually, then we will begin to truly behold the riches of God's glory for each one of us!

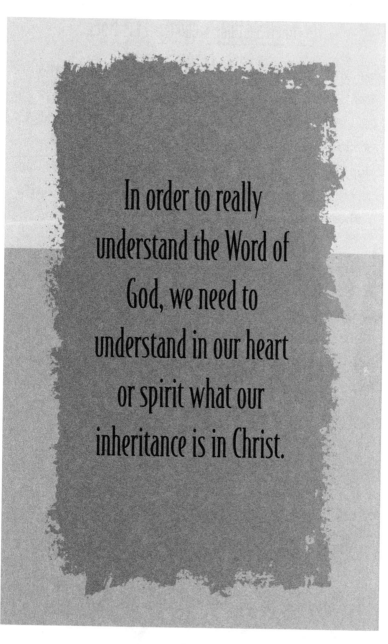

In order to really understand the Word of God, we need to understand in our heart or spirit what our inheritance is in Christ.

You've Become Complacent

FROM A PASTOR'S HEART

I'm concerned that many in the Church today are being rocked to sleep in the devil's cradle of complacency. Many believers have become complacent with their lot in life and have stopped diligently pursuing the things of God like they once did. They're no longer on fire to accomplish more for God's Kingdom or to change their circumstances with His Word. The things of God that once burned in their hearts have become commonplace to them.

But we should all be dissatisfied with complacency and refuse to allow it to hinder our walk with God. We should never entertain the idea of letting go of what God has told us to do. We should always be striving toward the mark of the high calling in God!

Friend, it's time we move forward with everything that's in us to do what God has told us to do. Time is short! Too many believers are just enjoying what God has given them while the rest of the world perishes. We can't afford to sit down and pat ourselves on the back and say, "Glory hallelujah! We've got it made!"

I thank God for all the benefits we have as Christians. I thank God for healing, prosperity, faith, and every benefit of our covenant in the Lord Jesus Christ.

Yes, God has given us those benefits to enjoy. But God didn't institute the Church just so we could have a good time! He commissioned the Church of the Lord Jesus Christ to take the Gospel to a world that's lost and dying. And it's time we wake up and obey that divine commission to do something with all the knowledge we've gained from the Word — we must reach the world for Jesus!

The enemy knows he can't destroy the Church from the outside, so he's tried to move in with his complacency and lull the church to sleep. We need to wake up! We must stop allowing ourselves to become so interested in enjoying the benefits of our faith that we lose sight of God's purpose for our lives.

If the Lord came for His Church today, how many souls would you take with you? Or would you just say, "Well, Lord, here I am. I made it in!" When the Master comes, you don't want to be one of those who has just been sitting around marking time. Be in that company of those who are sold out to do the will of God!

The Master of the harvest expects the Church to reap a harvest of souls for His glory! Are we really ready to meet Jesus?

We must stop allowing ourselves to become so interested in enjoying the benefits of our faith that we lose sight of God's purpose for our lives.

INSPIRED WORDS

CONCERNING

Victory

FOR THE SEASONS

OF YOUR LIFE

Encountering a Trial

FROM A PASTOR'S HEART

Many times when believers are confronted by problems that try to pull them off victory's mountain back down into the valley, they have a tendency to think they have done something wrong. But that isn't always the case.

God never said that when we begin to follow Him and to obey His Word, we would never have a trial. However, God did say that although many are the afflictions of the righteous, God would deliver us from them all (Ps. 34:19).

I think it would help us sometimes if we viewed our trials from a different perspective. If you are successful in God, you are going to face problems — the devil will see to that. The devil wants to block the path and prevent the progress of people who are doing something of value for the Lord.

249

The problems of life inevitably come to all of us. That's why it's important for us to make a conscious decision to view life's problems as *stepping stones* to greater victory and success, rather than to allow them to become *tombstones* to mark a place of failure and defeat.

Neither the circumstances of life nor the actions of others determine the course of your life. You alone — by your own response to obstacles that may come your way — determine whether or not you are a success. Actually it isn't even the obstacle, but your *attitude* toward it that determines whether you are an overcomer or a failure.

So many times when people are faced with problems or obstacles, they become overwhelmed and give up. But if you give up and quit when faced with opposition, you have turned the obstacle into a tombstone that will be a memorial to failure and defeat in your life.

In the face of seeming failure, hold your ground and say, "Mr. Devil, I will not stop! I will not quit. I refuse to turn around, and I will not give in." Then proceed to take that obstacle and turn it into a stepping stone to go to the other side — to the victory side.

If an obstacle is trying to block your path to victory, don't stop in front of it and accept defeat. Lift up your eyes to the One who is your Helper, and start walking right over the top of that obstacle saying what God's Word says about you. Begin to boldly declare: Greater is the Spirit of God that is in me than any obstacle that stands before me (1 John 4:4). Thanks be unto God who *always* causes me to triumph (2 Cor. 2:14).

You will find that when you act on the Word of God, the obstacles Satan intended to be tombstones to mark your defeat will instead become stepping stones along your road to victory in Christ.

Neither the circumstances
of life nor the actions of
others determine the
course of your life.
You alone – by your own
response to obstacles that
may come your way –
determine whether or not
you are a success.

Encountering Life's Difficulties

Amid life's uncertainties and the problems we face in the world today, we as Christians must make a decision to keep our trust and our faith in God and His Word.

When things go wrong in life, what do we do and to whom do we turn? What is our stand? Do we throw in the towel and quit, or do we press on in our Christian walk and remain faithful to God? These are questions that many don't want to deal with and that some refuse to face, because these issues involve maintaining faith in God through the hardships of life.

Problems, tests, trials, and disappointments in life are real facts, but a strong faith in God is the answer to every one of life's difficulties. We must realize that God has not promised us that we would never face a test or trial. But He has promised us that He would never leave us and that He would cause us to triumph, because He has overcome the world (John 16:33)!

The answer to life's problems is not to "hide our heads in the sand," hoping the problems will go away. Nor is the answer to question our faith in God. We must instead do as the Bible exhorts: *"Trust in the Lord with all thine heart; and lean not unto thine own understanding"* (Prov. 3:5).

Many have faced adversity in life, yet they maintained their faith in God. If you were to talk to some of these people, you'd find that they are stalwart men and women of God today — not because of their adversity, but because they chose to persevere. With their eyes fixed on Jesus, they came through the storm and discovered once again the calm that awaited them on the other side.

The ocean of life may not always be as smooth as glass. But through faith in God, we always have an anchor of hope to steady us and keep us on course. So when the storms of life assail, and everything appears to be going wrong, ask yourself, "Is not God still God? Or is He only God when things are going smoothly?" Purpose in your heart that the unchanging God is God at *all* times — when times are good and when times are difficult. In all places and under all circumstances, God is still God!

It's during the hard times that we need to dig our heels in the ground and make the decision, "I cannot be defeated, and I will not quit!" It's a decision that each of us has to make. We can allow the situations and circumstances of life to either bring us closer to God — to a place of confidence and certainty in Him — or drive us further away into the uncertainty and suffering of the world.

If you have been discouraged or have wavered in your faith, I encourage you to pick up the pieces of your disappointments and failures and make the decision to go on with God. Stand stronger on His Word than you ever have before! Rise up to your full stature in Christ, and be more determined than ever that victory belongs to you! The choice is yours. God is still God!

We can allow the situations and circumstances of life to either bring us closer to God – to a place of confidence and certainty in Him – or drive us further away into the uncertainty and suffering of the world.

Enjoying a New Life in Christ

"Therefore we are buried with him [Jesus] by baptism into death: that like as Christ was raised up from the dead by the glory of the Father, even so we also should walk in newness of life."

— Romans 6:4

Twenty-five years ago, a story appearing in the news shocked people throughout the nation. A 71-year-old woman, who weighed only 50 pounds and had begged door to door for food, died of malnutrition in a nursing home after spending the last few days of her life there.

When the authorities investigated her case they discovered that she had left behind a fortune. There was more than a million dollars of assets in two safety deposit boxes — $800,000 of the sum was in cash, and the remaining worth was in valuable shares of stock. She had such wealth at her fingertips, and she probably had enough money in that safety deposit box to buy the best restaurant in the whole city, yet she died because she didn't have enough to eat.

Some people might say, "She was a fool," but today, sitting in churches all over this nation and around the world, there are Christians who are just as foolish as she was. What do I mean by that? I mean that there are Christians who are living in spiritual poverty even though Christ has made them rich!

You see, whatever the Bible says belongs to us is ours — we're heirs and joint-heirs with Jesus Christ (Rom. 8:17)! Yet not all Christians avail themselves of the riches of Heaven that have already been put into their accounts through Jesus. The riches are available to them — all they have to do is open the safety deposit box, so to speak, pull out what they need, and start using it.

Yet there are many Christians today who are wasting away. And if they're not careful, they will die in a condition of spiritual, physical, mental, or emotional poverty. But it isn't God's fault if they live and die in that condition. It's their own fault, because they didn't use what God had already made available to them through the death and Resurrection of Jesus Christ. In the case of the lady who starved to death, no one but her had anything to do with her dying in that condition. And just like her, if people today don't enjoy the new life that Christ Jesus provides, it's not anyone's fault but their own.

When you received new life in Christ, you were given a new position in Him. You were made a new creature, a child of God, and a joint-heir with Jesus Himself (2 Cor. 5:17; 1 John 5:1; Rom. 8:17)! You need to learn to live in this new position and to receive all the benefits that go along with it.

Unfortunately, many Christians don't live at the level that they should, and many times it's because of guilt. They may realize that God in Christ has forgiven them for mistakes they made, but they have a hard time forgiving themselves. So they carry guilt around, not because God is laying it on them, but because they are laying it on themselves.

Our new position in life through Christ Jesus doesn't include any guilt. Romans 8:1 says, *"There is therefore now NO CONDEMNATION to them which are in Christ Jesus, who walk not after the flesh, but after the Spirit."* Remember, once you're born again, you have a new life and new position in Christ. All things have become new — the old things have passed away and don't exist anymore (2 Cor. 5:17)!

Sometimes, you may fight the memories of the past in your mind. The devil may keep bringing up the past — what you've done, how bad you've been, or how much you've messed up. Just stand on God's Word, and tell the devil, "I'm in Christ and I have a new position in Him; therefore, I have no condemnation or guilt. Go peddle your goods elsewhere, because you're not going to accomplish anything here!"

It's not your own spirit bringing those condemning thoughts, because your spirit is pure and free. And it certainly isn't God condemning you. It's just the enemy sitting on your shoulder, so to speak, whispering in your ear, and reminding you of past mistakes. But if you'll renew your mind with the Word of God, you'll get rid of any guilt or feelings of condemnation (Rom. 12:2).

Let's live this new life in Christ knowing that no outside force can separate us from God or keep us from receiving God's best (Rom. 8:35-39). The only thing that can keep us from receiving God's best is the person who stands in our own shoes. And once we have brought ourselves under control and are being led by the Holy Spirit, then there isn't *anything* that can keep us from living a victorious life in Christ!

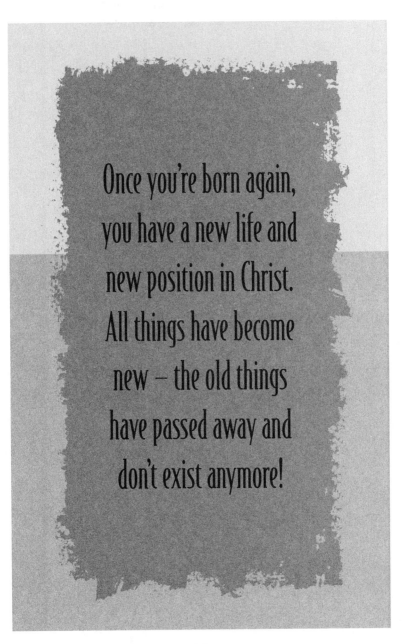

Once you're born again,
you have a new life and
new position in Christ.
All things have become
new – the old things
have passed away and
don't exist anymore!

Everything Goes Wrong

FROM A PASTOR'S HEART

What do we do when everything is going wrong? What do we do when someone doesn't receive healing? What do we do when a loved one dies?

These are questions many people don't like to deal with. But we must realize that God never promised us that we wouldn't face tests, trials, and adversity. We will all face problems in life, so we need to learn how to deal with them.

We can't hide our heads in the sand or ask "Why?" We must maintain our faith and trust in God and His Word. Then we must do exactly what the Word says: *"Trust in the Lord with all thine heart; and lean not unto thine own understanding"* (Prov. 3:5). If we lean to our own understanding, we lose sight of the fact that God is still God.

You have to make a choice. Is God, God all the time? Or is He just God when everything is going well and there's no adversity in your life? No! God is God at all times, in all places, under all circumstances — good or bad!

Adversities are setbacks, but they don't have to be victories for the enemy. For example, in Mark 6:5 Jesus went to His hometown, *"And he could there do no mighty work . . . ."* When Jesus experienced adversity, did He quit? No. He went around to the villages preaching and teaching and healing all (v. 6).

So what do we do? We do what Jesus did; we pick up the pieces and keep right on going with God, no matter what happens!

We live in this world, and the Bible says that the devil is the god of this world, who goes about as a roaring lion seeking whom he may devour (2 Cor. 4:4; 1 Peter 5:8). And occasionally something happens, and we face a tragedy. Do we pull back from a strong stand on the Word when we face adversity? No, we stand stronger, rise to our full height, check our armor, and go out more determined than ever to defeat the enemy!

In the natural, I have always been the kind of person who avenged a loss or defeat. For example, when I was in high school and lost a track race, the first thing I did was find out when my team was going to compete against that team again. I knew that runner would be in the same race again.

I set my sights and began to train harder. When the day of the race came, I lined up on the starting line and looked over at the runner who had beaten me before. Then I said to myself, *He will never beat me again.* And he didn't!

Bouncing back from tragedy or defeat is *our* decision. We must look forward with the attitude: "I may have lost a battle, but I will win the war!"

And we must go on with God. If we don't move on with God, we allow the devil to win the war. Our victory rests with us realizing that God is still God and His Word is still true — and always will be!

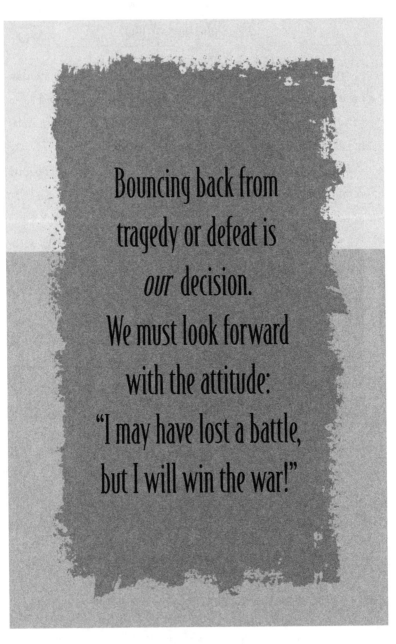

Bouncing back from
tragedy or defeat is
our decision.
We must look forward
with the attitude:
"I may have lost a battle,
but I will win the war!"

Going Up the Down Side of Life

FROM A PASTOR'S HEART

At times, we may feel as though we're going up the down side in life. Someone might say, "What are you talking about?" Let me give you an example. Have you ever tried to go up a down escalator? You might take two steps forward and fall back four steps. It takes tremendous effort to make it to the top.

Well, sometimes that's the way it is for believers. What should you do when you find yourself in that position? You will wear yourself out trying to go up the down side if you don't trust in God's Word.

When everything is going wrong, one of the first things we do is question whether or not we're in the will of God. But you know something, I have never seen the devil attack anyone who was out of the will of God. Why should he? The devil is not interested in stopping someone if that person is already out of the will of God.

So when I find myself in a test or trial, with the devil sitting on my shoulder hollering, "You better check; you're probably out of the will of God," I tell him, "This trial is the best sign I have that I'm *in* the will of God." I'm not saying that the problems are from God, because the devil is the one who causes problems for God's people.

God didn't say that you wouldn't have trials or tribulations, but He did say that He would bring you out on the other side with victory (Ps. 34:19)! So don't start trying to figure out where you went wrong, because the devil would love to tell you where you missed it.

But the devil isn't the only one who will tell you that you're defeated. People will say, "You're never going to make it. You shouldn't have tried in the first place."

That's why you need to renew your mind with the Word of God. When you know what the Word says, it won't matter what the devil or anyone else says or does or what your senses tell you — nothing will deter you! You're going to keep standing on the Word, and God will see you through!

When everything and everyone seems to be against you, remember that you "*. . . have overcome them: because greater is he that is in you, than he that is in the world*" (1 John 4:4). If the

Greater One is living inside you, why are you listening to the devil?

The Bible says that we are more than conquerors through Christ (Rom. 8:37). I want you to grab hold of that. We're not just *conquerors*. We're *more than conquerors*! Therefore, we cannot be overcome!

I'm not saying that you might not fail sometimes, but you're not a failure until you quit. So when you feel like you're going up the down side, put the Word of God to work in your life — keep standing on His promises — because it's not your wisdom or strength that will cause you to rise up in victory; it's God and His Word!

When you know
what the Word says,
it won't matter what
the devil or anyone else
says or does or
what your senses
tell you –
nothing will deter you!

Keeping Your Eyes on Jesus

". . . Let us run with patience the race that is set before us,
Looking unto Jesus the author and finisher of our faith; who
for the joy that was set before him endured the cross, despising the
shame, and is set down at the right hand of the throne of God."

— Hebrews 12:1,2

In the community where I live, many local organizations sponsor annual 5K and 10K races in which experienced and inexperienced runners can compete for a good cause. If I were watching one of those races, I could tell you after the first few minutes who will end up in front and who will bring up the rear.

Usually, the people who fall to the rear are the ones who are out there running just to be running. They're looking

271

around at everything, horse-playing with one another, grumbling, complaining, and even walking partway through the race. But it's the runners who are more focused who eventually finish in the lead.

It's not hard to spot a focused runner. He doesn't care what the other fellow is doing behind him or alongside him. He's not looking around to see who's watching him from the sidelines. No, he's looking straight ahead because he has a goal he's reaching for, and he is determined to make it to the finish line!

I used to run the hundred-yard dash on my track team in high school, and I know how important it is to stay focused in a race. I once saw a guy lose his event because his girlfriend yelled out his name from the grandstands and distracted him from his goal — the finish line. But from the time I would leave the starting blocks until the moment I'd cross the finish line, I'd fix my eyes way down the track and keep looking straight ahead at the goal before me. I knew if I looked around, it could cost me the race.

The Apostle Paul talked about our running the race that is set before us, *looking unto Jesus* (Heb. 12:2). You see, we are running a race — the race of life — and what we focus on will determine how we finish.

We can't afford to look at other people alongside us who are running *their* race. We can't allow ourselves to be distracted by the crowd of problems and circumstances that call out for our attention. We can't let the devil and his lies trick us into taking our eyes off the goal and cause us to lose our race. No, we have to keep looking at Jesus. As long as we keep our eyes on Him, we *will* finish our course!

So how are you running *your* race? What are *you* looking at? I want to encourage you to develop the same kind of determination in life that the track runner has out on the field. Stay focused. Keep your eyes on Jesus. Keep your eyes on the Word. Strive to reach the goals that lie before you, and don't let anything distract you.

Grit your teeth, set your jaw, and run with the attitude, "I've started out to run life's race for God, and I'm not letting up until I finish!" Then just keep your eyes on Jesus because He is the *Author* and the *Finisher* of your faith!

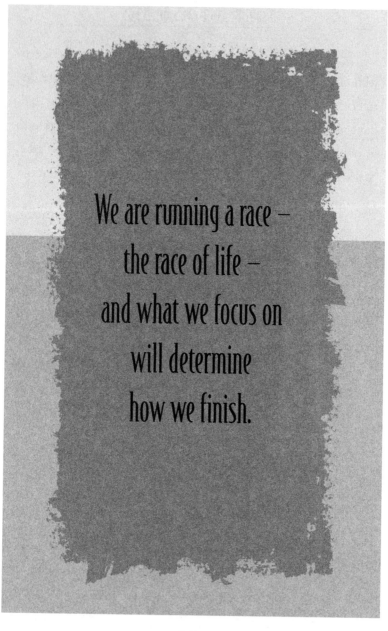

We are running a race —
the race of life —
and what we focus on
will determine
how we finish.

Needing Strength and Power

FROM A PASTOR'S HEART

"I can do all things through Christ which strengtheneth me."
— Philippians 4:13

Notice the first two words of this verse: "I can." Of course, in our own strength, we are nothing, but through Christ we can do all things. But if we don't believe we can do all things through Christ, we can't. That's why we must quit saying, "I can't!" or we will rob ourselves of the strength that Jesus provided for us — strength to do what we need to do in life.

I remember one of my grade-school teachers always saying, "Don't say you can't! If you keep saying you can't do something, you will believe it, and you won't be able to do it! Instead, say, 'I can do it!'"

If you don't believe in the power of God to help you succeed, you will never be able to accomplish anything worthwhile for God. You must believe in what God can do through you because you are in Christ.

My dad, Rev. Kenneth E. Hagin, always told me as a child, "With God, you can do anything and accomplish anything you desire in life." When the Bible says, "I can do all things through Christ," the "I can" is based on God, not on you. With God, you can accomplish any task set before you.

You see, when you abandon "I can't" and replace it with "I can," you are taking the first step in walking by faith. Then God will help you do what you cannot do in your own strength, ability, and wisdom. God will meet you when you take a step of faith. But as long as you stand still doing nothing, saying, "I can't!" God has nothing to bless!

Notice the first part of Philippians 4:13: *"I can do all things . . . ."* Not *some* things. Not a *few* things. But you can do *all* things! You see, you can do all things in Christ, not because of *who* you are, but because of *whose* you are. Your confidence and strength come from God, not from you.

Some people never do anything for God because they are afraid of failing. But I would rather be considered a failure for trying than to be a failure because I never stepped out in faith to do something for God.

I tell people who stumbled and failed, "You are only a failure as long as you stay on the ground. Get up, dust yourself off, and go on with God!"

The last part of Philippians 4:13 says, ". . . *through Christ which strengtheneth me.*" The secret of your strength and overcoming power is in Christ. It's not *your* strength and ability; it's *His.* You will be amazed at what can be done when you believe in the power of the One who lives on the inside of you!

Jesus Christ is the Source of your strength. Stop looking to yourself to overcome the enemy or to have the wisdom to know what to do in life! You are strongest in life when you are totally dependent upon God. Your strength comes from obeying God's Word and doing what God told you to do.

Continually remember that your power source is not limited to what you can do. But with God as your Helper, your power source is unlimited! Therefore, you can say with authority, "I can do all things through Christ who gives me the power!"

Neither the circumstances of life nor the actions of others determine the course of your life. You alone – by your own response to obstacles that may come your way – determine whether or not you are a success.

Obtaining the Prize

"I press toward the mark for the prize of the high calling of God in Christ Jesus."

— Philippians 3:14

Discipline. It seems almost everybody enjoys hearing the success stories of others — about the rewards and benefits of discipline, training, and hard work. But many don't care to hear about the *discipline* part of success.

No one has ever become successful in business, in sports, or in any area of life who has not disciplined himself in some way to achieve his goals. For example, no football player has ever made it to the top in his field without working out on a consistent basis, studying and memorizing plays, and then playing with all his heart and soul on game day! That kind of discipline is the fuel that kindles the fires of success!

One definition of discipline is *training that develops self-control and acceptance or submission to authority*. I like that definition! We can apply that to our own lives as Christians. We discipline or train ourselves in the things of God by continually bringing ourselves into submission to the authority of God's Word. When we accept God's Word as final authority and allow it to govern our actions, we enable ourselves to reap the rewards and benefits of walking in line with the Word.

Success in life is not an overnight process, and it doesn't always come easy. Any successful person will tell you that. But he will also probably tell you that his success was well worth the discipline, perseverance, and self-control he had to practice over a period of time to achieve his goal.

Discipline is the fuel that kindles the fires of success, but it is also *the bridge that carries a person from his dreams to his destiny!*

I like the saying "Discipline is *remembering what you want.*" Jesus Christ underwent the disciplining of His flesh in His earth walk as He proceeded from the Garden of Gethsemane to Pilate's Judgment Hall and, finally, to Golgotha's Hill. The Bible says He could have called upon twelve legions of angels to deliver Him from that old rugged cross, the Cross of Calvary (Matt. 26:53), but Jesus remembered what He wanted! He remembered you and me and a lost and dying world that would be able to partake of redemption through the finished work of the Cross.

Certainly the temptation to give up and quit was hard on Jesus' flesh! Going to the Cross was no easy task! Yet for you and me — the joy or prize set before Him — Jesus persevered in the will of God and was rewarded (Heb. 12:2).

There is a great lesson for us to learn in Jesus' fulfilling the will of God and obtaining the prize of redemption for all mankind. So let us look unto Jesus as we press toward the prize of God's calling for our own lives! Let us discipline ourselves according to the Word to achieve our God-given goals and dreams. We can enjoy success after success in every area of our lives if we will dare to pay the price of obtaining the prize!

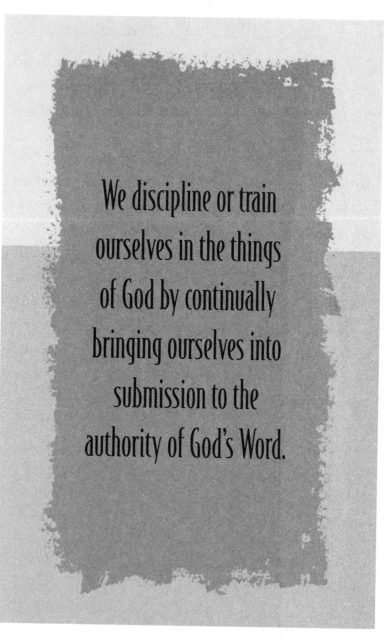

We discipline or train
ourselves in the things
of God by continually
bringing ourselves into
submission to the
authority of God's Word.

Overcoming Problems

T The world we live in is full of people who have troubles — and we Christians are not excluded! Yet some believers think that when they start living by faith, it's as though they've taken some sort of spiritual antidote that makes them immune from any kind of trial or circumstance. Other believers try to act as if they never have any problems. They think that if you admit you're having trouble, you're not in faith.

Well, there's something wrong with those ideas, because the Bible warns us that we *will* have tests and trials. First Peter 4:12 says, *"Beloved, think it not strange concerning the fiery trial which is to try you, as though some strange thing happened unto you."* Then Psalm 91:15 says, *"He [the believer] shall call upon me [God], and I will answer him: I WILL BE WITH HIM IN TROUBLE; I WILL DELIVER HIM, and honour him."*

Many other scriptures also tell us to expect trials (Ps. 34:19; James 1:2). Yes, problems do exist, but we can overcome them! The secret is talking to God about our problems.

Some people take their troubles to a preacher, doctor, lawyer, or friend. They say, "I've just got to talk to someone." I wonder why they don't talk to God first. It's okay to talk to someone else about your problem, but no one can give you lasting help like God can!

The Bible says that Jesus is touched with the feeling of our infirmities (Heb. 4:15). I want you to notice that He was tempted like we are, yet He didn't sin.

Some believers, even though they haven't sinned, still feel guilty or condemned because they were tempted. One man said, "Well, if you were tempted, you might as well have done it." That doesn't make sense. You can't keep a bird from flying over your head. But you sure can keep him from landing on your head and building a nest! Similarly, since the devil is the god of this world, you can't stop evil thoughts from coming to you. But you don't have to think or dwell on them. You can *resist* them! If you have trouble resisting, just tell God and He will help you.

When an evil thought or temptation comes to your mind, don't say, "Oh, I guess I really messed up. I've blown it now." You haven't blown it just because thoughts come to your mind or temptations come along. It's when you think on those evil thoughts and act on them that the problem starts.

You would be surprised to know how many people think that they're the only ones who have been tempted in a certain way. Some people tell me, "I'm probably just so different from everyone else." I say, "Really? First Corinthians 10:13 says, *'There hath no temptation taken you but such as is common to man . . . .'* So you see, you're not different!"

The devil wants you to think that no one understands or has ever been through what you're going through. If he can get you to start thinking in that vein, you won't talk to God. When you don't tell God what your problem is, He can't help you. But if you will pray and tell God all about your problems, He will give you direction, deliverance, and victory — just as He promised in the Word!

Since the devil is the
god of this world,
you can't stop
evil thoughts from
coming to you.
But you don't have to
think or dwell on them.
You can *resist* them!

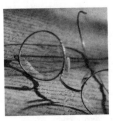

Receiving the Promises of God

FROM A PASTOR'S HEART

"*And if ye be Christ's, then are ye Abraham's seed, and HEIRS ACCORDING TO THE PROMISE.*"

— Galatians 3:29

You are an heir of God! In fact, the Bible says in Romans 8:17 that if you are born again, you are a joint-heir with Christ. So you need to ask yourself the question, *Am I living like an heir?*

Well, what is an heir? First of all, an heir is one who succeeds another in the possession of property, title, office, wealth, fortune, or resources. You are not an heir until someone has left you something.

If you understand the New Covenant, you know that Jesus Christ has left you a glorious inheritance! Ephesians 1:18

says that God has given you the riches of His glory in Christ as your inheritance. Think about that!

What does this mean to you personally? It means that you have certain rights and privileges in Christ, and you need to find out what they are. In fact, to a great extent the success of your Christian life is measured by understanding who you are in Christ, what you possess in Him — and then by taking advantage of what belongs to you!

How do you find out what belongs to you? An inheritance is usually stated in a will. The Word of God — the promises of God — contains God's will and testament, telling you what you have inherited. All the promises of God tell you what your rights and privileges are in Christ. They have already been given to you through Jesus. But now it is up to you to receive the promises of God so you can live your life in the fullness of your inheritance.

No one is going to force you to receive your inheritance in Christ, not even God Himself. Of course, He wants you to receive what belongs to you, but He won't come down and force you to receive the riches of His glory in Christ.

You could become an heir today and inherit a million dollars, but unless you *take advantage* of what belongs to you, you could live on the street, homeless, without a penny in your pocket. You could actually live in dire poverty, even though you have in your possession the title deed to a mansion and a savings account totaling a fortune!

Yet this is what we do all the time when it comes to the things that belong to us in God. We may even pull the Bible out, look at all the promises of God, and say, "I am an heir! The Lord promised me this in His Word," yet never actually receive any of those promises in our lives.

You may have a deed to your home or a rental agreement of some kind. If someone tried to move into your home or apartment, you wouldn't just tell your family, "It looks like we are going to have to move out!" No, if you have legal documents proving your right to be there, you are going to stay and tell the intruder to leave!

You can do that because you know what belongs to you, and you know what your rights are. Yet what do you do when the devil walks in and starts taking advantage of you by bringing his sickness, lack, poverty, and trouble? Do you just let him have his way, or do you stand against him with the Word?

You must take your stand on the Word for what belongs to you! You need to tell Satan, "Devil, I am an heir! This belongs to me! In the Name of Jesus, leave now!"

It is up to you whether or not you ever receive the promises of God in your life. It is up to you whether or not you live in the freedom that belongs to you as an heir of God! You can allow the devil to take advantage of you, or you can rebuke him and put him in his place. Then stand your ground and begin claiming all the wonderful promises of God that already belong to you as an heir in Christ

To a great extent
the success of your
Christian life is measured
by understanding who
you are in Christ,
what you possess in Him –
and then by taking
advantage of what
belongs to you!

Staying Prepared

B

". . . Be instant in season, out of season . . . ."

— 2 Timothy 4:2

My grandfather was a farmer, and he was very sensitive to certain times and seasons of the year. For example, he could recognize the least little sign that pointed to a coming change in the weather. One time Grandpa started telling everyone: "We're going to have an early spring this year." And although it was still cold outside, he and his workers went out into the fields to break up the dry ground to get it ready for planting seed.

Grandpa's neighbor didn't believe what he'd said. But when the weather changed suddenly, that neighbor hustled and bustled for two weeks trying to get his equipment ready. He finally did get his seed into the ground, but because he was so late getting started, he missed out on reaping a bumper crop that year!

Well, if you're not careful, the same thing can happen to you spiritually. You may be progressing along in your daily routine, not being as sensitive as you should be to the Holy Spirit's promptings. Then all of a sudden something happens — your situation changes — and you're not prepared! So what do you do?

If you're like some folks, you begin to scurry around, confessing the Word and grabbing hold of God's promises, trying to catch up on lost time. But how much better off you would be if you were already prepared for the change — if you were instant in season *and* out of season!

Now certainly you can expect to enjoy refreshing times in the Presence of the Lord if you're obeying the Word and doing what God tells you to do (Acts 3:19). But times of refreshing are not something you dwell in continually. They're seasonal.

Thank God for seasons of refreshing. But you just can't live for those times. You have to be prepared for other seasons too!

I know in my own personal life that some of the greatest trials and tribulations I've had to face came right after times of great refreshing.

If you remember, something similar happened to the prophet Elijah. His greatest season of despair came after a tremendous season of rejoicing. The people were holding him in high esteem because he'd just called down fire from Heaven and had the false prophets of Baal put to death.

But just a few hours later, Elijah's season changed, and Jezebel's pursuers were after *his* life. So Elijah took off, running scared like a whipped puppy. And he ended up sitting under a juniper tree, feeling helpless and despondent (1 Kings 18:21-40; 19:1-5).

That may describe your situation today. Maybe you were shouting the victory just two weeks ago, but now you're sitting under a "tree of despair" because your rent is due, your car is breaking down, there's no food in the pantry, and your paycheck is already spent!

Well, what are you going to do? Are you going to give in to despair? No! Get up, shake yourself out of your despondency, and act as if the Word is true, because it is! The same God who is with you in the times of refreshing is the God who will see you through every trial and tribulation!

It's easy to float along through life when you're "in season" — when all of your needs are met, and everything is going fine. The real challenge is keeping the victory when your season changes!

As long as you live, seasons will come and go. But God and His Word will never change. So just stay with God and His Word, and you'll have everything you need to stay prepared both *in season* and *out of season!*

It's easy to float along
through life when
you're "in season" –
when all of your needs
are met, and everything
is going fine.
The real challenge is
keeping the victory when
your season changes!

Tempted to Waver

" . . . *Be thou strong and very courageous, that thou mayest observe to do according to all the law, which Moses my servant commanded thee: TURN NOT FROM IT TO THE RIGHT HAND OR TO THE LEFT, that thou mayest prosper whithersoever thou goest.*"

— Joshua 1:7

With the Promised Land before them, the children of Israel didn't have time to be wishy-washy followers of God, believing God one minute and complaining against Him the next. Their fathers before them did that and died in the wilderness without obtaining the promise. They were not victims of the circumstances that opposed them; they were victims of their own unbelief.

Years later under the leadership of Joshua, the same opportunity for possessing the Promised Land awaited a new generation of God's people. God commanded the Israelites to believe His Word and to obey it "not turning to the right hand or the left." Obedience to God's Word would ensure their victory. And as this second generation of Israelites trusted and obeyed God, they entered the Promised Land and obtained their long-awaited inheritance.

You and I have an inheritance that was purchased by Jesus Christ's own blood in His substitutionary work on the Cross. But whether it be the baptism in the Holy Ghost, healing, financial prosperity, deliverance from a bad habit, or *any* blessing that belongs to us in Christ, obedience to God's Word is the key to possessing our inheritance and winning the victory.

Hebrews 12:2 says, *"Looking unto Jesus the author and finisher of our faith; who FOR THE JOY THAT WAS SET BEFORE HIM endured the cross, despising the shame, and is set down at the right hand of the throne of God."* Do not follow the example of the first-generation Israelites, who through unbelief were prevented from entering their Promised Land (Heb. 4:6,11). Instead, follow the example of Jesus, the Author and Finisher of your faith, and fix your gaze on the joy set before you — the promise of your inheritance in Christ.

Don't give up on your miracle! By looking unto Jesus, you can march steadily toward your own promised land and overcome any circumstance that tries to oppose you or distract you from your goal. If you will believe and hold fast to God's promises, you *will* receive your miracle from God.

By looking unto Jesus,
you can march steadily
toward your own promised
land and overcome any
circumstance that tries to
oppose you or distract
you from your goal.

Triumphing in Christ Jesus

"*Now thanks be unto God, which always causeth us to triumph in Christ . . . .*"

— 2 Corinthians 2:14

Newspaper, radio, and television news reports make us keenly aware that we live in a world that is bound for utter defeat and destruction. They also make us aware of the fact that man cannot extricate himself from all the troubles, trials, and tribulations that surround him.

Man is limited, but God has made a way for us to enjoy peace, liberty, happiness, and victory. At times, darkness and distress may seem to be overtaking us, but "*. . . thanks be unto God, which ALWAYS CAUSETH US TO TRIUMPH in Christ . . .*" (2 Cor. 2:14).

The Apostle Paul said that God *always* causes us to triumph — not an occasional victory followed by a group of defeats, then another victory. No! *God always causes us to triumph!*

I want you to understand that this statement was made about people whose faith in God has no limits! Faith brings you to the reality of victory over every circumstance that stands in the way of your success.

Remember when Paul and Silas were in jail with bleeding backs, locked in the innermost part of the prison? It looked like it was all over. But they prayed and began to sing a song of victory. As they sang, every prison door was opened, every captive was set free, and the jailer was brought to his knees in repentance when he saw the miracle-working power of God (Acts 16:22-33)!

Real faith always brings the realization of victory and never defeat! Someone said, "Oh, it sounds too good to be true. Preacher, you'd better watch it. You're giving them too much hope. Remember, we live in a world where we don't know what may happen tomorrow."

No. I don't know what's going to happen tomorrow in the world. But I know what's going to happen with me, because the Word of God says that I always triumph in Christ Jesus! The economic world may fall apart, and food may become scarce, but I will never fear because God is my source! And God said that I would always triumph — no matter what comes or goes!

In the face of every obstacle that shouts, "It can't happen," we need to stand strong and say, "You say it can't happen. But the Bible says '. . . *If thou canst believe, all things are possible to him that believeth*'" (Mark 9:23)!

The world can't believe it. They only see the whipping post, the shackled feet, and the iron prison door. The world never understands the song of victory in the midnight hour. It makes no difference what prison you're locked in — spiritual death, financial despair, sickness and disease — you can be delivered!

Maybe the reason you aren't seeing victory is because you're looking at the circumstances. You're looking at what has you trapped instead of acting on your faith.

Too many people are waiting for God to do something, but God is waiting on them. For example, the children of Israel stood helpless and in despair with the Red Sea in front of them and the Egyptian army behind them. They cried out to the Lord, then ". . . *the Lord said unto Moses, Wherefore criest thou unto me? speak unto the children of Israel, that they go forward: But lift thou up thy rod, and stretch out thine hand over the sea, and divide it: and the children of Israel shall go on dry ground through the midst of the sea*" (Exod. 14:15,16).

God didn't say, "Stretch out your rod and *I'll* divide the sea." He told *Moses* to stretch out *his* rod and divide the sea!

If you're in a similar situation today, God is saying the same thing to you: Go forward! You need to get hold of the fact that *you* have to do something. God has already done all He's ever going to do.

Someone said, "You mean *I* have to do it?"

Yes! The power of God will be manifested when you put some action to your faith.

In our own strength, we are limited. But in God there is no limit! We *can* triumph. Jesus Christ has already purchased victory for us, but you and I must do something about it. If you will dare to believe God, act in faith, and step out on the promises of God, you will triumph!

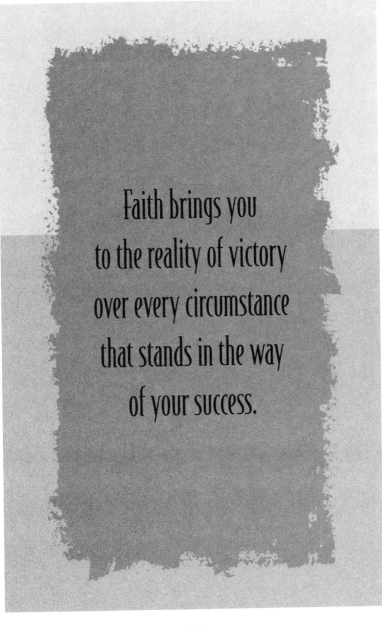

Faith brings you
to the reality of victory
over every circumstance
that stands in the way
of your success.

You Are Offended

A good memory is an important attribute to develop. The ability to recall what you have learned or experienced in the past can often serve you well in the future. However, there are times when it is best to cultivate the ability to *forget*.

As we go through life, opportunities to become offended will invariably arise. Whether we are confronted with thoughtless words or unkind acts, each of us will face situations and circumstances that have the potential to hurt, insult, or even devastate us in one way or another. The results of such wounds and offenses can last a lifetime — unless, of course, we *choose* to forget.

Have you ever met a person who had been offended or who had suffered an injustice from someone years ago, yet that person continued to recall the incident as though it had just happened? Although the incident was past tense, it still affected that person's present state of mind.

But regardless of how painful an experience or how malicious a person may have been toward us, we will only benefit in life if we choose to forget the offense. By setting our expectation upon God and not upon man, we can afford to forget wrongs we have suffered. We know that God is on our side and that He will always cause us to triumph and be victorious in Christ (2 Cor. 2:14).

Joseph is an example of a man who was blessed because he chose to forget what he had suffered. Joseph was sold into slavery by his own brothers, thrown into prison because of false accusation, and forgotten by someone he had helped in a time of crisis. If anyone ever had sufficient reason to become disillusioned, depressed, and bitter, it was Joseph. But in the midst of great persecution and personal distress, Joseph didn't become bitter; Joseph became better.

Joseph allowed the fiery trial of persecution to burn away the impurities in his own soul. Instead of constantly thinking on the wrong others had done, Joseph busied himself with doing what was right. And the scriptures tell us that whatever he did prospered because "... *the Lord was with Joseph, and shewed him mercy, and gave him favour* ..." (Gen. 39:21).

In the midst of his suffering, Joseph maintained strong fellowship with God. He continued to sharpen both his natural skills of organization and administration, as well as his spiritual skill of interpretation — explaining the divine will of God through dreams.

When Joseph was finally summoned by Pharaoh to assume the position he was destined to occupy, Joseph was better equipped to fulfill that role than he would have been when he first dreamed of it. But Joseph would not have been so well-equipped and qualified had he chosen to hold a grudge against those who had mistreated him.

We hinder ourselves from making progress in the future when we allow ourselves to become enslaved by remembering the past. But we put ourselves in position for God to promote His plan in our lives when we forget the past. For example, Joseph chose to look beyond his suffering to behold the glory God had promised. Consequently, all that God had promised Joseph did indeed come to pass. After Pharaoh appointed Joseph the ruler of his kingdom, Joseph said, ". . . *For God . . . HATH MADE ME FORGET all my toil, and all my father's house . . . God hath caused me to be fruitful in the land of my affliction*" (Gen. 41:51,52).

When Joseph's brothers discovered his identity, they became fearful that he would seek vengeance. But Joseph revealed the character his sufferings had forged. Joseph displayed character that qualified him for the task appointed him when he said, "*. . . be not grieved, nor angry with yourselves, that ye sold me . . . . God sent me before you . . . to save your lives by a great deliverance. So now it was not you that sent me hither, but God . . .*" (Gen 45:5,7,8).

It may not seem easy to forget a heartache, a false accusation, or an unkind act. But you can forget the wrong which men commit against you when you remember the good God has performed for you.

David, too, was a man well acquainted with disappointment and persecution. But in Psalm 103:1 and 2, David gives us an example of what we should not *forget*: "*Bless the Lord, O my soul: and all that is within me, bless his holy name. Bless the Lord, O my soul, and FORGET NOT ALL HIS BENEFITS.*"

Despite persecution or perhaps even personal failure, we can follow the example of Joseph and David. We can emerge victorious from any test or trial by choosing to forget the pain caused by men and choosing rather to remember the blessings of God.

It may not seem
easy to forget a heartache,
a false accusation,
or an unkind act.
But you can forget the
wrong which men commit
against you when you
remember the good God
has performed for you.

You're Not Making Any Progress

FROM A PASTOR'S HEART

If you're like most shoppers, you want to get the best deal for your money, especially when you make a major purchase. For instance, if you need a car, you probably won't just run out and buy one. You'll stop first, look around to see what's available, and listen to what the different dealers have to offer to make sure you don't get taken advantage of.

Well, that doesn't make just good economic sense; it makes good *spiritual* sense too. In other words, you can use the same logic — to stop, look, and listen — to keep the devil from taking advantage of you.

You see, a lot of Christians are living as though they're on a spiritual roller coaster. They're up today and down tomorrow. Others always seem to be on a merry-go-round. Nothing

315

ever changes. They go around day in and day out living in defeat, and they *stay* in defeat.

But God doesn't want you to be an up-and-down Christian, and He certainly doesn't want you going around in circles, making no progress in your Christian walk. He wants you to keep moving forward in Him!

So every once in a while, it's good to just *stop* and *look*. Look at what? Look at yourself. Take inventory of your life, and examine your spiritual condition. Check to see if you're headed in the right direction in your walk with the Lord. And the way you do that is by looking at yourself from God's perspective.

It doesn't do you any good to just look at yourself from the natural standpoint. You also have to look at yourself from the Word of God, because the light of His Word causes you to see the areas of your life that need to be changed. Looking at the Word will also help you find real solutions to life's problems.

Have you ever heard someone say that when you walk by faith, you'll never have any more problems or trials? Well, the Bible says that tests and trials are going to come to all of us (John 16:33). But we can always come out of them victoriously by looking at God's Word instead of looking at the problems.

Look at God's Word, and you'll see that He has already forgiven your sins. He's already healed your diseases. He's already provided for all your needs. And He's already made a way for you to triumph in the face of adversity!

But it's not enough just to *look* at the Word and see your benefits. You have to *listen* to the Word too! I'm not talking about just hearing the Word with your ears, because you can hear the Word and never do anything about what you hear. I'm talking about really *listening* to the Word — hearing it, comprehending it, and acting on what it says (James 1:22-25)!

So I just want to encourage you to take time out to examine yourself. See what the Word has to say about you and your situation; then act on what you see. If you'll be a doer of the Word and not just a hearer of it, the Word will direct you and change you.

Don't let the devil talk you into settling for less than God's best. And don't allow yourself to get stuck in a rut, riding spiritual roller coasters and merry-go-rounds all your life. Just remember to *stop*, *look*, and *listen*, and you can experience God's blessings and walk in victory!

It doesn't do you any good
to just look at yourself
from the natural standpoint.
You also have to look at
yourself from the Word of
God, because the light of
His Word causes you to see
the areas of your life that
need to be changed.